Southern

Traditions

Southern Traditions

◆

A Seasonal Cookbook

◆

Margaret Agnew

Photographs by Sylvia Martin

VIKING STUDIO BOOKS

VIKING STUDIO BOOKS
Published by the Penguin Group, Penguin Books USA Inc., 375 Hudson Street,
New York, New York 10014, U.S.A.
Penguin Books Ltd, 27 Wrights Lane, London W8 5TZ, England
Penguin Books Australia Ltd, Ringwood, Victoria, Australia
Penguin Books Canada Ltd, 10 Alcorn Avenue,
Toronto, Ontario, Canada M4V 3B2
Penguin Books (N.Z.) Ltd, 182–190 Wairau Road,
Auckland 10, New Zealand

Penguin Books Ltd, Registered Offices:
Harmondsworth, Middlesex, England

First published in 1994 by Viking Penguin,
a division of Penguin Books USA Inc.

1 3 5 7 9 10 8 6 4 2

LIBRARY OF CONGRESS CATALOGING-IN-PUBLICATION DATA
Agnew, Margaret Chason.
Southern traditions: a seasonal cookbook / Margaret Agnew;
photographs by Sylvia Martin.
p.   cm.
ISBN 0-670-84393-8
1. Cookery, American—Southern style.   2. Southern States—Social
life and customs.   3. Menus.   I. Title.
TX715.2.S68A37   1994
641.5975—dc20   93-39217

Printed in Singapore
Set in Perpetua
Designed by Kathryn Parise

*To the Chasons, the Callaways, the Agnews, and the Rutlands for
their support and wonderful family recipes.*

◆

To my husband, Bob, for his patience and encouragement.

◆

*To my son, Robert, for helping me to see new beauty
in the world around me.*

Contents

Winter ✦ Come in from the Cold

Spring ✦ Outdoors at Last

Summer ✦ Catching a Breeze

Acknowledgments

I would like to thank the following people for their contributions to *Southern Traditions*:

Elizabeth Taliaferro, for her help in testing recipes and preparing food for photography; her pleasant smile made this a happy project.

Sylvia Martin, whose skillful photographs captured the feel of the South; taking such a large number of photographs is no small feat, especially when it is crucial to capture each season at its peak.

Marjorie Johnston, for finding so many wonderful props and locations for the food photographs; we would have been lost without her unique style and flair.

Susan Noble, for helping us discover the hidden treasures of Mississippi.

Catherine Hamrick, for supplying just the right word whenever I was stuck.

My family and friends were always ready to lend a helping hand or pose for a photograph: Rex Bowman, James Brindley, Anne-Marie Brown, Beth Gundersen, Mary Emma Jefferson, Jeff Johnston, Miles Kimbrell, Lucy Montiel, Walker Morris, Gene Murphree, Beverly Rutland, Helen Rutland, Eva Royal, Winn Shannon, Scott Smallwood, Norval Springfield, and Linda Wright.

My gratitude also goes to all the homeowners across the South who so graciously shared their homes for photography, but especially to Laura Abernethy, Laurie Alverson, Yates Amason, Robert Anderson, Barbara Ashford, Alvah Barron, Leslie Byars, Mary Ann Byers, Elizabeth Campbell, Jean Carraway, Richard Chadwick, Emy Christian, Caroline Clark, Kathryn Cloud, John Conway, Mrs. William Cooper, Mary Catherine Crowe, Geraldine Culp, Susan Curtin, Ann Daniels, Barbara DeBank, Beth Dillard, Bingham Edwards, Merlyn Foster, Jacquelyn Gage, Judy Gaiser, Trisha Griess, Brenda Hackney, Mary Hallmark, Edna Heard, Carolyn Hill, Anne Holbrook, Marjorie Johnston, Betty Lankford, Mrs. William Lum, Mrs. Gene McLain, Emily Major, Barbara Manning, Mary Mellen, W. B. O'Neal, Isabella Person, Jane Person, Jeanne Rogers, Alice Schleusner, Lynn Schuppert, Mrs. John Sparkman, W. D. Spradlin, Barbara Stone, Hazel Swanson, Nelson Taylor III, Susan Tipler, Mary Margaret Todd, Cathrine Tubb, and Josephine Tucker.

I am indebted to the following special people, places, and organizations who are actively involved in preserving bits and pieces of our Southern heritage: Attic Antiques (Birmingham), The Ballastone Inn (Savannah), Doris Ann Benoist, Linda Bishop, E. R. Blanchard, Amy Blyth, Frank Bradley, Ann Brittain, Dan Brooks, Loveta Byrne, Callaway Gardens, Helene Crozat, Bobby Debleaux, Jeanette Feltus, Edward Fryzel, Tim Hargus, Fran Harold, Betty Hertzog, Historic Charleston Foundation, Julie Hudson, John Humphrey, Cathy Jenkins, Cynthia Jenkins, Carrol Kay, Hugh Lineberger, Lucinda Mays, Joanne Mitchell, Natchez Pilgrimage Garden Club, Donna Owens, Mary Louise Patterson, Francis Pressly, Frank Richardson, Grace Roberts, Maxine Southerland, Pat Spring, Jenny Stacy, George Trask, Alice Van Trease, TwoSuns Inn (Beaufort, South Carolina), Betsy Veronee, Janet Waters, Wild Dunes Beach Resort (Charleston, South Carolina), Wisteria Antiques (Birmingham), and Connie Wyrick.

Special thanks go to my agent, Jean Naggar, who knew immediately how to turn my ideas into a book; to Michael Fragnito, my publisher, for believing in me; and to Barbara Williams, my editor, for always listening patiently to my concerns. And last, but certainly not least, to Kathryn Parise for designing this beautiful book; she made my vision become a reality.

Introduction

It is only natural that I love the South, for I have lived there all my life. My childhood was spent in Bainbridge, Georgia, a small community built around a downtown park. Later, we moved to Tallahassee, Florida, a cosmopolitan college town with a constant influx of new faces. My adult life has centered on Birmingham, Alabama, a bustling city of tall buildings, freeways, and fine old homes.

My own family is made up of Southerners—the Chasons and the Callaways. My father's family identified with the rural farming life in south Georgia. He knew the joy of an afternoon dip in the river and the inconvenience caused by a heavy spring rain on red clay roads. My mother's family settled in north Florida. She enjoyed whiling away summer evenings on the front porch in a rock-

Left: Guests to this home in Eutaw, Alabama, must enter through a pointed picket fence and gate. The gateposts are patterned after the columns across the front of the house. ♦ *Below left: A simple wooden plank hung by ropes from a backyard tree can provide hours of pleasure for a small child.*

ing chair and warmed herself by a large stone fireplace in the living room on winter nights.

When I married, my husband introduced me to more Southerners—the Agnew family from northwest Georgia, and the Rutlands from northwest Alabama. His parents had married and settled in Decatur, Alabama, a quiet cotton town with pretty homes built on fertile Tennessee Valley soil.

I began work on this book long ago. I can remember, even as a child, marking time by seasonal celebrations. Fall meant it was time for the school year to start, time for football games, Halloween, and a large Thanksgiving meal. I counted on winter to make an appearance by Christmas and to stay through February; I was occasionally delighted by a rare short-lived snow. Spring was welcomed by a fresh palette of pastel colors in the garden and on our Easter dresses. Summer meant the end of school, days on the beach, and Fourth of July fireworks.

I have traveled through every state in the South during all four seasons. This travel allowed me to create a lasting picture in my mind of the land, its people, its food, and its seasons. I have many wonderful memories of my travels. I remember a warm Sunday afternoon in Highlands, North Carolina, when visitors strolled up and down the main street, stopping to window-shop or to purchase an ice cream cone. I remember the sun setting as a covey of quail settled along the wide, flat Tennessee River, and the endless hills rising and falling in north Georgia. I remember the lacy wrought-iron porches of New Orleans, the pink dogwoods in Greenville, South Carolina, and the majestic homes of Natchez, Vicksburg, Selma, and Eufala.

I also have many wonderful memories of Southern food. Each time I slide my chair to the dining table, I am reminded of the bountiful Sunday meals my mother would prepare. After a morning of Sunday school and church, she would loop an apron over her head, and in no time a platter of crispy fried chicken and bowls of mashed potatoes, green beans, and sliced tomatoes would appear. This seemingly effortless meal would be topped off with thick slices of pound cake or tangy lemon meringue pie and plenty of iced tea.

These meals weren't really effortless, of course. But my mother was like so many other Southern mothers who put thought and love into what they served their families. They knew how to plan ahead, to bake from scratch, to cook what was in season, and to pickle and preserve when there was an abundance of figs, cucumbers, peaches, tomatoes, or strawberries. They thought nothing of rising early to make biscuits for breakfast. They insisted on a garden for fresh vegetables and herbs, and would drive miles to find the best blackberry patch.

Food was important to my family, and most of our group activities involved food. Whenever my aunts, uncles, parents, and grandparents gathered for an outing to the coast, we looked forward to having a fish fry. We would spend most of the day fishing for flounder, grouper, or croaker. By late afternoon my grandfather would have his large cast-iron skillet heated, ready to fry the catch. I'll never forget the taste of those cornmeal-coated fish—moist and flaky on the inside, crisp and crunchy on the outside.

Food is the language that ties Southern communities together. Whenever there is a festival or contest, folks collect around an open-pit fire to take turns flipping quarters of chicken, pork shoulders, or ribs. There are bags of boiled peanuts, frosted coconut cakes, peanut butter cookies, and sweet potato pies for sale.

Early Southern farm life also revolved around food and the growing seasons. Whether they gathered to grind grain, to marry, to bury the dead, to barter, to play games, or to pray, food was always at the center of a farmer's life. As a result, food began to symbolize Southern hospitality.

The tradition of Southern hospitality—sharing large quantities of good food and drink with friends and strangers—has proved to be enduring. If there was ever an ultimate gathering spot in the Southern home, it was surely the dining room, for this is where guests were greeted with the finest their hosts could offer.

On the great plantations, the food in the mansion dining room was far more elaborate than in the houses of most ordinary Southerners. Meals for slaves might have been prepared in the central kitchen, but more probably, their meals were cooked in their cabins in a pot in the fireplace. The slaves had a great influence on Southern food. From them came dishes using okra, black-eyed

There are great pleasures to be found in the solitude of winter. This is the time to be inside, with family, and plan for a spring that is sure to come.

peas, collard greens, yams, and benne seeds. They originated the recipe for beaten biscuits and a long list of impressive desserts.

The aftermath of the War between the States and the Great Depression left the South poor. Food was scarce and times were hard. With almost no money for food, homemakers had to be resourceful. They taught each other what they knew about cooking. They learned how to make a rich gravy from fat and flour, how to turn stale bread into pudding, and how to stretch a minimum of vegetables into a soup or stew. They planted, harvested, cooked, baked, canned, and preserved what they could.

Today some Southerners are concerned that modernization and a rising New South might dilute our heritage. That is why we must take time to study our "foodways." It is important to remember that our food tells a story about us; it tells others who we are. We must continue to keep alive our distinct heritage and traditions so they can be passed along to future generations. Our great Southern food is too wonderful to forget.

So get ready; let's take a journey through the seasons of this great region, and sample a taste of what the South is all about.

Fall

Coming Home

Fall brings a carpet of colored leaves and pumpkins

waiting in the fields. The senses rise to fragrant apples and

breezy days and cool, damp nights. Festivals and fairs

pass the time and the harvest moon hangs low

behind tall pines.

Above left: The giant sunflower has been popular for generations with Southern gardeners. These profuse daisy-like flowers bloom for weeks, and because they grow so tall, they can easily become the center of attention in

𝓕all has a tendency to ease across the South, flirting with the senses. The first hint of the season usually comes in late August. A breeze, lighter than a fingertip, touches the neck, lifting summer heat and humidity for just an instant. Though dog days hang on into September, this gentle wind promises cooler weather.

Several weeks later the pace picks up under the spell of fall. The high school band practices

autumn gardens. ✦ *Center and right: Billowy clusters of lavender-blue ageratum, giant sunflowers, and goldenrod are attractive in fall flower beds and meadow gardens. Their weedlike appearance is part of their natural charm.*

every afternoon, and the beat of drums energizes the neighborhood. Windbreakers, buried in the closet for months, must be donned for brisk walks before sundown. Overhead, migrating birds sound off. Some fly on, but old friends—cardinals, blue jays, mockingbirds, and sparrows—stay. Their calls are reminders to refill bird feeders.

The sky hangs clear and blue, and the wind

blows crisply, nipping a little pink into cheeks. Calendars are pulled out in anticipation of an October weekend in the mountains, when nature will paint the trees with her boldest palette—flaming red, rich gold, and orange. Now is the time to enjoy the soaring color, for all too soon this beauty will flutter to the ground.

While leaves are changing colors, some Southern sportsmen pull on their hunting gear and head for the woods to bag their first game meal of the season. They return home to cook such delicacies as fried quail with cream gravy and marinated duck breasts.

In hilly areas, the apple harvest is taken in hand by energetic cooks, who prepare apple pies, applesauce, apple butter, apple jelly, apple cider, and apple dumplings. In the middle and lower South, owners of muscadine vines begin to pick the plump purple or bronze grapes, ready to preserve the intense fruity flavor in jellies, preserves, sauces, and wines.

Above left: An old ox yoke hangs above the doorway of this small Appalachian log barn. ♦ *Below: Bales of hay dot a hillside that is surrounded by a vast array of fall colors. This serene, scenic vista is typical of many found along the roadsides of the Great Smoky Mountains.*

Left: Alvin York Mill is located ten miles north of Jamestown, Tennessee, on the Wolf River. The mill, built during the 1870s, featured a screw-type turbine wheel that ground grain for corn-meal and flour until 1940. ♦ Below: It is not unusual during the fall season to see people in pecan fields, dragging burlap bags behind them, combing the ground for the prized nuts. Some-times farmers will package the nuts in bags and sell them from small roadside stands.

By mid-October, children become anxious to visit nearby pumpkin fields to select the largest ones for jack-o'-lanterns. The smaller, easier-to-handle pumpkins are reserved for pies and cakes.

Travels down country farm roads lead us past pecan groves with wide-spreading trees symmetrically set in the earth. Beneath the bare branches, pickers collect the prized nuts, dropping them in rough burlap sacks. Later, the nuts will be shelled and the meat pulled from within and turned into pies, candies, cookies, and cakes.

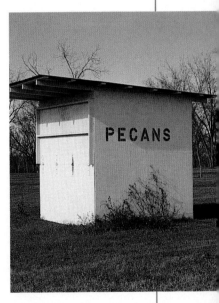

This season heralds a time of fellowship. We return home to renew ties with parents, brothers and sisters, aunts and uncles, grandparents, and cousins. We gather for Thanksgiving and its riches—roast turkey, dressing, and sweet potato pie made from family recipes handed down from mother to daughter. Fellowship can be as simple as steaming bowls of chili shared at the kitchen table on Sunday night.

How we savor this season, its changes, its rituals, and its bounty—tailgate picnics, ruddy apples, pumpkins, Halloween, pecan pies, and the joy of sharing them with loved ones! It is truly a harvest of experiences.

The Fall Garden

The fall flower garden is lush and colorful. There are plenty of frilly cosmos—a wondrous sight whether they're white, pink, gold, or purple. Brightly colored salvia, chrysanthemums, sunflowers, and goldenrod are also spectacular. But in the fall, the real action takes place in the vegetable garden, where greens, cabbage, and sweet potatoes are at their peak.

The South has never lacked for greens—turnip greens, collard greens, mustard greens, kale, and others. Most families tell of per-

Opposite: Synonymous with fall, the chrysanthemum is a glorious addition to fall gardens. The flowers are often classified according to the shape and arrangement of the blossom petals: pompom, spoon, quill, spiders, anemone, decorative, incurved, or cushion. ♦ Inset: Mexican bush sage is a type of salvia that blooms in the fall. In fact, it is spectacular during late September, October, and November, when it sends up long, slender spikes of a uniform deep rose-purple color. This salvia furnishes good cut flowers and looks nice when used in a garden border. ♦ Above: The cosmos is the ideal flower for gardeners who are seeking an abundant supply of autumn blossoms that are equally good for cutting and outdoor display. White, pink, gold, or purple cosmos are available; the mature height can range from three to six feet.

snickety mothers and grandmothers who thoroughly washed and inspected every leaf before cooking. Some folks call that stage of preparation "looking the greens." The greens are cooked for two hours or so in a big cast-iron pot, along with a "streak o' lean and streak o' fat" (bacon or fatback) for flavor. For many, the quintessential Southern meal includes a "mess" of turnip greens in tasty pot likker (turnip-green broth) with steaming corn bread, pork chops, sliced onions, and hot pepper sauce.

Some cooks like to slice the white turnip roots and cook them with the greens. Others cook turnip roots as they would rutabagas— peeled, diced, then cooked in a little water until tender. Pepper, salt, and butter are all that's needed for seasoning.

If you can't get enough turnip greens, you're sure to like kale, a

Top: This fall garden full of ornamental cabbage yields a harvest of colorful leaves for arrangements and garnishes. Although it is possible to eat these bright leaves, their flavor is inferior to that of culinary cabbage. The cabbages should stay pretty until the temperature drops below freezing. ♦ Center: In the South, turnips are grown as much for their greens as for their roots. The turnip is a popular fall vegetable, especially when a light frost has made the greens taste a little sweeter. Purchased fresh from a farmer or at the market, turnips are often bound together with rough twine to form a "mess" of greens. ♦ Right: Before the cabbage plant begins to form a head, it looks similar to a collard. The cabbage is ready to harvest when the head feels firm and solid.

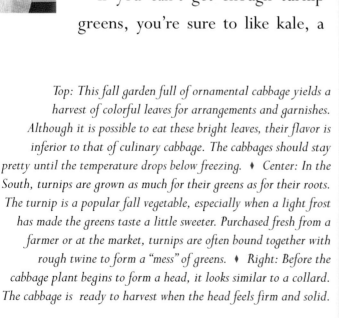

Right: Southerners often refer to sweet potatoes as yams, but the fact is, very few yams are marketed or sold in this country. This confusion has come about because of the need to distinguish our dark orange-skinned sweet potato from the light yellow-skinned sweet potato of the North. The Southern sweet potato has a vivid orange, sweet flesh that cooks to a soft, moist texture. The potatoes are considered a fall crop, and are harvested before the first frost. After harvesting, it is best to cure the potatoes for at least five to ten days in a dark, warm place. ♦ Below right: Curly-leafed mustard greens are one of the prettiest vegetables in a fall garden. Planted in late summer, the bright greens reach full size in only four to six weeks. The young leaves are mild enough to eat raw in salads; the larger leaves tend to have a stronger flavor and are best cooked.

hardy, pretty plant with leaves edged with delicate ruffles. Kale is a cool-weather vegetable and can be planted from seed in late summer in rows or beds. If kissed by the frost, kale leaves will taste sweeter. You can cook kale as you would turnip greens, although not quite as long; some cooks will add a little sugar. Others like to cook the two vegetables together to mingle the flavors.

Cabbage also catches its share of attention in the fall, even before harvest. The outer leaves grow large and free, tinged with purplish veins, and smaller leaves fold around the center. You can grow cabbage from seed in early August, but it's easier to start with small plants in late summer. Set them in rows about twelve to eighteen inches apart.

There are two traditional ways to cook this vegetable: shredded and fried in a skillet with bacon grease or chopped and boiled with salt pork.

Sweet potatoes have always been a major item on Southern menus. From the time they are harvested in late summer until as long as they last into winter, they appear on the table boiled, baked, candied, fried, or made into pudding or pie. A hot sweet potato topped with a pat of butter is an especially delectable dish.

A Harvest of Fruit

Every Southerner warmly remembers apple recipes handed down in the family. Cider often tops the list, with its enticing scent of cloves and cinnamon. Before the advent of supermarkets, country folks would use a press that squeezed the juice from the apples. In a matter of days, the juice would ferment to perfection.

The easiest recipe, apples dried in the sun, is also extraordinarily flavorful. But apple butter was, and still is, a mountain favorite.

Opposite: Muscadines are harvested when they are fully ripe, usually from late August to October. When ripe, the scuppernong and Fry varieties take on a bronze color; the Thomas and Pride varieties will be black. ♦ Inset: Apples can be harvested once they reach a desirable size. Because of our warm Southern climate, red apples will not always be of an outstanding color, but the taste is nonetheless excellent. Good cooking apples include the Red Rome, Stayman Winesap, and Granny Smith; for fresh eating, select a Golden Delicious, McIntosh, or Granny Smith. ♦ Above: Apples are traditionally a Northern crop, but they are grown, to a lesser degree, here in the South. North Carolina and Arkansas both have major commercial apple industries. In addition, there are several crabapple farms dotting the hills of north Alabama and north Georgia. Most of the harvesting of these trees is done by hand, usually from September through October.

Above: Muscadines make an excellent accent for the garden when used as a trellis or border. Here they are pretty trained onto a one-wire trellis about five feet above the ground. ♦ *Below left: Bright orange pumpkins, bales of hay, and dried cornstalks make attractive fall decorations.*

Made with stewed apples sweetened with spices, this thick golden-brown sauce is best when spread on an open-faced buttered biscuit or dinner roll.

Novice cooks delight in baking apples swimming in cinnamon-and-sugar syrup, while the more experienced indulge their families in golden-crusted cobblers, tarts, dumplings, and pies.

Some Southerners are lucky enough to have a few muscadine vines growing in their yards. The vines are often trained to grow on a fence, arbor, or trellis, giving the garden a charming, old-fashioned look. These native Southern grapes—purplish black or bronze-colored—are especially beautiful in the early morning, shining with dew.

By fall harvest, the grapes hang in rich clusters, ready to be picked and eaten out of hand or put up as jellies, preserves, sauces, and wines. Muscadine jelly spread on a steaming, just-split biscuit is a wonderful treat.

Southerners have been making homemade wine with muscadines for years. The grapes have an intense fruity flavor and a somewhat musky odor, which probably explains the origin of their name. Records show that Thomas Jefferson was very fond of scuppernong wine made in North Carolina. He maintained that the wine would hold its own on the best tables of Europe and that it had a fine aroma and appearance.

In some parts of the South, pumpkins are so plentiful in the fall that no good cook would ever consider using the canned product rather than selecting a fresh one straight from the field.

The largest, prettiest pumpkins make the best jack-o'-lanterns, but most cooks agree that smaller pumpkins (those weighing two to three pounds) are better for cooking because their flesh is more tender and they contain less water. Fresh pumpkin is tasty mashed and baked with a brown sugar glaze or stirred into breads, pies, cookies, puddings, and cakes.

Below: An October visit to Had Too Orchard near Vinemont, Alabama, provides a look at thousands of pumpkins destined to be carved into Halloween jack-o'-lanterns. W. D. Spradlin, owner of the orchard, says he sells most of his crop to markets in Alabama and Georgia.
♦ Right: Halloween and pumpkins go hand in hand. These stuffed Halloween people are part of an amusing display of pumpkins spotted in rural western Alabama.

Fall Recipes
Cooking Up Tradition

FISH AND SHELLFISH

Fall is the best time for seafood, especially along the coasts of Florida, Alabama, Louisiana, and Mississippi. As gulf winds begin to cool, snapper, mullet, flounder, crabs, shrimp, and oysters become more plentiful and more flavorful than at any other time of year. Bridges and piers host amateur fishermen, who cast out their lines, hoping to bring home dinner. Professional fishermen depart in large boats before daylight and return late in the afternoon, having tonged up oysters or hauled in nets brimming with shrimp or baskets filled with crabs. Closer to shore, fishermen wade knee-deep to throw small nets, trapping mullet as they jump in the sparkling tide.

At home the fish and shellfish might be worked into a spicy gumbo or jambalaya. But most of the time the seafood receives very simple treatment—steaming, frying, poaching, or baking.

Mullet Sandwiches

Fresh mullet, fried or made into sandwiches, is often served at seafood festivals along the Gulf Coast. This sandwich uses flaked mullet, but you could substitute almost any firm, light-colored fish.

For poaching fish:
>   1 pound mullet or other fish fillets
>   3 cups water
>   2 tablespoons lemon juice
>   ¼ teaspoon salt
>   ¼ teaspoon black pepper
>   ⅛ teaspoon cayenne pepper
>
>   3 hard-cooked eggs, chopped
>   ½ cup pimiento-stuffed olives,
>   chopped
>   ⅓ cup mayonnaise
>   3 tablespoons chopped green onions
>   1 tablespoon grated horseradish
>   ¼ teaspoon salt
>   ¼ teaspoon black pepper
>   6 (6- to 7-inch) whole-wheat French
>   bread loaves, sliced lengthwise and
>   lightly toasted
>   Lettuce leaves

Combine fillets, water, lemon juice, salt, black pepper, and cayenne in a small fish poacher or large skillet; bring to a boil. Cover, reduce heat, and simmer for 7 to 8 minutes, or until fish flakes easily when tested with a fork. Drain well. Remove skin from fish; flake fish with a fork.

Combine flaked fish, eggs, olives, mayonnaise, onions, horseradish, salt, and pepper, stirring gently. Chill. Spread French bread loaves with mullet mixture. Add lettuce leaves and close sandwiches. Cut sandwiches in half if desired.

Yield: 6 servings.

Fresh mullet is best when you buy it directly from coastal fishermen, but it can also be purchased at the fish market. After poaching, the fish is flaked and turned into Mullet Sandwiches.

Florida Crab Dip

This creamy baked seafood dip is popular in the panhandle area of Florida. It's simple, but delicious!

½ pound fresh crabmeat, drained and flaked
1 (8-ounce) package cream cheese, softened
1 (3-ounce) package cream cheese, softened
1 tablespoon milk
1 to 2 tablespoons chopped green onions
1 to 2 tablespoons grated horseradish

Preheat oven to 350° F.

Combine crabmeat, cream cheese, milk, onion, and horseradish, mixing well; place in a small baking dish. Bake for 15 to 20 minutes, or until top is lightly browned. Serve hot with crackers.

Yield: 2 cups.

Fresh crabmeat is combined with cream cheese, green onions, and horseradish in Florida Crab Dip. The postcards are some that I collected as a child on family vacations.

Louisiana Jambalaya

There are many different versions of jambalaya, but they all seem to include three main ingredients—rice, pork, and seafood. The recipe below makes a filling main dish with just the right amount of hot, spicy flavor.

1 pound smoked sausage, cut into thin slices
1 cup chopped green bell pepper
½ cup chopped onion
½ cup chopped celery
2 cloves garlic, minced
1 tablespoon all-purpose flour
1 (28-ounce) can tomatoes, undrained and coarsely chopped
2½ cups water
2 cups regular long-grain rice, uncooked
1 teaspoon salt
½ teaspoon dried thyme leaves
¼ teaspoon black pepper
¼ teaspoon cayenne pepper
1 pound shrimp, peeled and deveined

Cook sausage in a large Dutch oven until browned. Drain off all but 2 tablespoons pan drippings. Add green pepper, onion, celery, and garlic; cook over low heat until vegetables are tender. Add flour, stirring until blended. Stir in tomatoes and water; bring to a boil. Add rice, salt, thyme, black pepper, and cayenne. Return to a boil, reduce heat, and simmer, covered, for 20 minutes. Add shrimp; cover and cook 5 minutes more, or until shrimp turn pink.

Yield: 8 to 10 servings.

Louisiana Jambalaya is a hearty one-dish meal the whole family will enjoy.

Coastal Gumbo

In New Orleans restaurants you can always count on gumbo being on the menu. This spicy seafood stew has a roux base and is thickened with okra.

¾ cup vegetable oil
¾ cup all-purpose flour
2 cups chopped onion
2 cups chopped green bell pepper
1 cup chopped celery
2 cloves garlic, minced
1 pound smoked sausage, cut into thin slices
1 pound okra, sliced
5 cups chicken broth
3 cups water
2 cups peeled, chopped tomatoes
1 (8-ounce) can tomato sauce
3 tablespoons Worcestershire sauce
1 bay leaf
1 to 2 teaspoons hot sauce
1 teaspoon cayenne pepper
¼ teaspoon salt
¼ teaspoon white pepper
½ teaspoon dried thyme leaves
½ teaspoon dried oregano leaves
1½ pounds medium-size shrimp, peeled and deveined
1 pound fresh grouper fillets, skinned and cut into 1-inch pieces, or
¾ pound fresh crabmeat, drained and flaked
1 (12-ounce) container fresh oysters, undrained
Hot cooked rice

Combine oil and flour in a large Dutch oven; cook over medium heat, stirring constantly, until roux is dark brown (20 minutes). Stir in onion, green pepper, celery, and garlic; cook 30 to 40 minutes, stirring frequently, until vegetables are tender. Set aside.

Cook sausage in a large skillet until lightly browned; drain, reserving 2 tablespoons drippings in skillet. Add sausage to vegetable mixture. Cook okra in sausage drippings over low heat until browned. Add to the pot, stirring well. Cook over low heat until thoroughly heated. Add chicken broth and water, stirring well. Add tomatoes, tomato sauce, Worcestershire sauce, bay leaf, hot sauce, cayenne, salt, white pepper, thyme, and oregano; reduce heat, and simmer 1½ to 2 hours, stirring occasionally.

Add shrimp, fish or crabmeat, and oysters to the pot with the vegetables and sausage. Simmer 15 to 20 minutes, or until edges of oysters begin to curl and fish is done. Remove and discard bay leaf. Serve gumbo over rice.

Yield: 10 to 12 servings.

This field, along-side the Blue Ridge Parkway, is filled with leafy cabbages. Farmers in this area produce much of the South's cabbage crop, which is generally harvested by mid-November. Most of it will go directly to market; the rest will be processed for slaw and sauerkraut.

VEGETABLES AND SALADS

You know the fall harvest is in when roadside stands begin popping up along the highways advertising apples, rutabagas, turnips, cabbages, and potatoes. All these fruits and vegetables make hearty additions to cool-weather meals.

Faced with such abundance, it is sometimes difficult for shoppers to make their selections. So here are some suggestions that capture the season's rich, robust flavors.

Sweet Acorn Squash Rings

Acorn squash ripens on the vine and is harvested in the fall. Its dark green shell and golden flesh make it a beautiful addition to the dining table.

1 large acorn squash
½ cup orange juice
½ cup firmly packed brown sugar
⅓ cup light corn syrup
¼ cup unsalted butter or margarine
1 tablespoon grated orange rind
¼ teaspoon ground cinnamon
⅛ teaspoon salt

Preheat oven to 350° F.

Remove stem from acorn squash and cut squash into ¾-inch-thick slices; remove and discard seeds. Arrange squash slices in a lightly greased 13- x 9- x 2-inch baking dish. Pour orange juice over squash. Cover with foil and bake for 35 minutes.

Meanwhile, combine rest of ingredients in a small saucepan. Bring mixture to a boil; reduce heat and simmer, stirring constantly, for 5 minutes, or until sugar is dissolved and mixture is slightly thickened.

After squash has baked, remove foil and pour sugar mixture over the squash. Return to the oven and bake an additional 15 to 20 minutes, or until squash is tender.

Yield: 4 servings.

Sweet Acorn Squash Rings make a striking addition to fall dinner tables. The rings are delicious served alone, but they could also double as the holder for a serving of peas, green beans, or cranberries.

Apple Orchard Salad

Selecting a favorite eating apple is strictly a matter of taste. You may like the sweetness of a Golden Delicious or prefer the full flavor of a McIntosh or the tart firmness of a Granny Smith. The best part of this salad is that you can combine several selections for one great flavor.

> *2 large green apples, cored, unpeeled, and diced*
> *1 large red apple, cored, unpeeled, and diced*
> *3 tablespoons lemon juice*
> *½ cup chopped celery*
> *½ cup raisins*
> *½ cup chopped pecans, toasted*
> *¼ cup mayonnaise*
> *1 teaspoon sugar*
> *Lettuce leaves*

Sprinkle apples with lemon juice and toss gently to coat; drain.

Combine apples, celery, raisins, and pecans, tossing gently. Combine mayonnaise and sugar, stirring well. Add mayonnaise mixture to apple mixture and stir gently. Serve over lettuce leaves.

Yield: 6 servings.

Traditional Turnip Greens with Turnip Roots

The worst part about preparing turnip greens is having to wash them. After that, it's sheer pleasure. In fact, some Southerners can make an entire meal out of a bowl of turnip greens with pot likker and a wedge of corn bread.

> *5 pounds young and tender fresh turnip greens with roots (1 large bunch)*
> *½ pound salt pork, cut into 4 pieces*
> *2 cups water*
> *1 dried red pepper pod*
> *½ teaspoon salt*
> *1 teaspoon sugar*
> *Hot pepper sauce (optional)*

Wash turnip greens thoroughly; drain and wash again. Drain well. Tear greens into bite-size pieces. Peel turnip roots and coarsely chop.

Rinse salt pork. Combine salt pork, water, pepper pod, and salt in a large Dutch oven over high heat; bring to a boil. Cover, reduce heat, and simmer 30 minutes. Remove and discard pepper pod. Stir in turnip greens; cover and cook 20 minutes. Add turnip roots and sugar; cover and cook 15 to 20 minutes, or until the greens and roots reach the desired degree of doneness. Remove and discard salt pork. Serve turnips with hot pepper sauce, if desired.

Yield: 6 to 8 servings.

Spoon up a helping of Traditional Turnip Greens with Turnip Roots, add some hot sauce, and you have a delicacy enjoyed by most Southerners. In the old days, turnip greens were cooked until they were practically mush, but modern cooks have shortened the cooking time in order to end up with greens that are not only greener but also have more flavor.

Glazed Rutabaga

Fall brings a harvest of rutabagas bursting with a distinctive flavor that Southerners love.

*1 large rutabaga, peeled and cut into
    cubes (5 to 6 cups)*
4 cups water
¼ cup unsalted butter or margarine
¼ cup firmly packed brown sugar
2 tablespoons lemon juice
1½ teaspoons Worcestershire sauce
¼ teaspoon salt
Cracked black pepper

Combine rutabaga and water in a large skillet. Bring to a boil; cover, reduce heat, and simmer 25 to 30 minutes, or until tender. Drain well.

Melt butter in skillet; stir in brown sugar, lemon juice, Worcestershire sauce, and salt. Add rutabaga; cook over medium heat, stirring constantly, 3 to 4 minutes, or until rutabaga is glazed and thoroughly heated. Sprinkle with cracked black pepper before serving.

Yield: 4 to 6 servings.

Creole Cabbage

Blue Ridge farmers produce much of the South's cabbage crop. Harvested as late as November, the leafy green heads are delicious steamed and topped with butter or, as here, simmered with tomatoes, onions, and green bell pepper.

2 slices bacon, cut into 1-inch pieces
¾ cup chopped onion
¾ cup chopped green bell pepper
*1 (28-ounce) can whole tomatoes,
    undrained and chopped*
1 medium head cabbage, chopped
¼ cup cider vinegar
½ teaspoon salt
½ teaspoon black pepper
3 dashes hot sauce

Cook bacon in a Dutch oven over medium-high heat until crisp. Add onion and green pepper; sauté until vegetables are tender. Add tomatoes, cabbage, vinegar, salt, pepper, and hot sauce. Cover and bring to a boil; reduce heat, and simmer 20 to 25 minutes or until cabbage is tender, stirring occasionally.

Yield: 8 servings.

A glaze made with brown sugar and lemon juice adds just the right amount of sweetness to Glazed Rutabaga.

Cades Cove, located on the western edge of the Great Smoky Mountains National Park, about eight miles from Townsend, Tennessee, is home to Cable Mill, built in 1868. This mill operated well into the twentieth century, with grinding millstones turning corn and wheat into daily staples of cornmeal and flour. The old waterwheel, fed by water from Forge and Mill creeks, continues to turn beside the mill structure.

BREADS AND SPREADS

Close your eyes and listen to water gushing through the overshot wheel of a grist mill. With a little imagination, you can step back to a time when our ancestors brought their fall corn harvest to the local mill to be ground into meal and flour.

Southern cooks have long claimed that fresh-milled flour yielded some of the best homemade bread in the world. This claim may be challenged by some, but the following traditional quick and yeast breads are certainly outstanding. Steaming corn bread, biscuits spread with muscadine jelly or apple butter, and sugar-glazed cinnamon rolls are among our most memorable offerings.

Country Corn Bread or Corn Sticks

Southerners eat corn bread all year long, but it is especially good when it accompanies fresh fall and summer vegetables. This recipe will make a round skillet of corn bread, a square pan of corn bread, or a dozen or so cob-shaped corn sticks.

1½ cups cornmeal
⅓ cup all-purpose flour
2 teaspoons baking powder
½ teaspoon baking soda
1 teaspoon sugar
½ teaspoon salt
2 eggs, beaten
1½ cups buttermilk
¼ cup vegetable oil or bacon
  drippings

Preheat oven to 450° F.

Combine cornmeal, flour, baking powder, soda, sugar, and salt, stirring well. Combine eggs, buttermilk, and oil; add to cornmeal mixture, stirring just until moistened.

Place a well-greased 8-inch cast-iron skillet, 8-inch square pan, or cast-iron corn-stick pan in oven for 4 minutes, or until hot. Remove pan; spoon batter into pan, filling corn-stick pan three-fourths full. Bake at same temperature for 15 to 20 minutes, or until lightly browned.

Yield: 6 to 8 servings, or 1½ dozen corn sticks.

Almost every cook has an opinion about what makes good corn bread. Some like to use self-rising cornmeal, some prefer to add flour or sugar, and some swear that a cast-iron skillet or corn-stick pan is the only pan in which to bake it. But one thing is for sure, a big piece of Country Corn Bread is an excellent companion to fresh vegetables.

VARIATION: Some cooks like to stir cracklings (pieces of pork fat that have been cooked until crisp) into their corn-bread batter to make cracklin' bread. For this recipe, use 1 cup cracklings.

Southern Spoon Bread

Traditional spoon bread is soufflé-like on the top and moist on the bottom.

2 cups milk
3 tablespoons unsalted butter or
  margarine
½ teaspoon salt
1 cup cornmeal
¾ cup water
3 eggs, separated, at room temperature

Combine milk, butter, and salt in a medium saucepan; bring to a boil over medium heat. Gradually add cornmeal, stirring constantly with a wire whisk. Remove from heat. Gradually add water, stirring well. Pour into a mixing bowl.

Beat egg yolks until thick and lemon-colored. Stir one-fourth of the hot mixture into the yolks; add tempered yolks back into the bowl with the remaining hot mixture, stirring constantly. Beat 3 egg whites with an electric mixer on high speed until stiff peaks form; gently fold into cornmeal mixture using a wire whisk. Preheat oven to 375° F. Pour mixture into a greased 2-quart casserole. Bake, uncovered, for 30 minutes, or until a knife inserted in center comes out clean. Serve immediately.

Yield: 6 to 8 servings.

Southern Spoon Bread looks like a soufflé, but the texture is much more dense. It can be served as a bread, or topped with a sauce of ham, tomatoes, or gravy.

Muscadine Jelly

Muscadines, or scuppernongs, are a variety of grape unique to the Southeast. They have a sweet flavor and a musky odor. I can remember my mother making muscadine jelly, a treat the whole family enjoyed.

3½ pounds muscadines (about 7 cups)
½ cup water
7 cups sugar
1 (3-ounce) package liquid pectin

Remove stems from grapes. Wash, sort, and place in a Dutch oven. Mash grapes by hand with a potato masher, a small amount at a time; add water. Bring mixture to a boil; cover, reduce heat, and simmer 20 to 30 minutes. Remove from heat, and press mixture through a jelly bag, extracting 4 cups juice. Cover and let cool completely.

Strain juice through cheesecloth into a large Dutch oven. Add sugar; stir well. Place over high heat; cook, stirring constantly, until boiling. Add pectin; return to a full boil; boil 1 minute, stirring constantly. Remove from heat, and skim off foam with a metal spoon.

Ladle hot jelly into hot sterilized jars, leaving ¼ inch of headspace; wipe jar rims, cover at once with metal lids, and screw on bands. Process in boiling-water bath 5 minutes.

Yield: 6 to 8 half pints.

Angel Biscuits

These biscuits are so light and fluffy they seem more like rolls than biscuits. Be sure to try them cut open and filled with thin slices of country ham or spread with Appalachian Apple Butter (page 35) or Muscadine Jelly (page 33).

2 packages active dry yeast
¼ cup warm water (105° to 115° F.)
2 cups buttermilk
5 to 5¼ cups all-purpose flour
¼ cup sugar
1 tablespoon baking powder
1 teaspoon baking soda
¾ teaspoon salt

1 cup solid vegetable shortening
¼ cup melted unsalted butter or
*   margarine*

Combine yeast and warm water in a small bowl; let stand 5 minutes. Stir in buttermilk and set aside.

Combine remaining dry ingredients in a large bowl; cut in shortening with a pastry blender until mixture resembles coarse meal. Add buttermilk mixture, stirring with a fork until dry ingredients are just moistened. Turn biscuit dough out onto a lightly floured surface, and knead 2 minutes.

Roll dough out to ½-inch thickness; cut with a 2½-inch biscuit cutter. Place biscuits on a lightly greased baking sheet and brush tops with melted butter. Cover with a cloth or towel and let rise in a warm place (85° F.), free from drafts, for 1 hour.

Preheat oven to 400° F. Bake for 10 to 15 minutes, or until biscuits are browned.

Yield: about 2 dozen.

Most biscuits are leavened with baking powder or baking soda, but Angel Biscuits are extra light because they also contain yeast.

Appalachian Apple Butter

Appalachian folks from West Virginia to Alabama traditionally cooked apple butter outdoors in a black kettle over a fire. We modern cooks still cherish the flavor of this sweet spread but have simplified the cooking process.

1 dozen medium-sized cooking apples, peeled, cored, and coarsely chopped
1 ½ quarts apple cider
⅓ cup red cinnamon candies
1 ⅓ cups sugar
1 tablespoon cider vinegar
1 ½ teaspoons ground cinnamon
½ teaspoon ground cloves

Combine apples, cider, and candies in a Dutch oven. Bring to a boil; cover, reduce heat, and simmer 1 hour, or until apples are tender. Drain apples; mash by hand with a potato masher, or spoon into a food processor and pulse just until smooth. Return mashed apples to Dutch oven, and add sugar, vinegar, cinnamon, and cloves. Cook, uncovered, over medium heat for 45 to 50 minutes, or until thickened, stirring often.

Remove from heat; ladle apple butter into hot sterilized jars, leaving ¼ inch of headspace. Wipe jar rims clean, and cover at once with metal lids; screw on bands. Process in a boiling-water bath 10 minutes.

Yield: 5 to 6 half pints.

Displayed across the top of an antique cupboard, jars of Appalachian Apple Butter wait to be opened and spread between steaming biscuits and dinner rolls.

Large native pecan trees grow wild along rivers and streams in Arkansas, Louisiana, Mississippi, and Tennessee. But pecan development companies are responsible for starting large pecan farms, such as this one in south Georgia. The pecan trees produce an excellent crop, but they are also useful as landscape and shade trees. You will find pecan trees gracing yards and homes across the South.

DESSERTS

During the fall harvest, farmers rise early and come home late. Harvesting peanuts and pecans, picking apples and pears, and digging sweet potatoes is rewarding but tiring work. Wise Southern farm wives add a little fun to this backbreaking work by cooking mouth-watering desserts that are taken to the field for lunch or served later at night. Raw peanuts are roasted and stirred into cakes or cookies. Pecans are toasted for candies. Apples and pears are peeled and sliced for tarts and turnovers. Sweet potatoes are mashed to fill flaky pastries. And on rare occasions a little bourbon is stirred into cake fillings and frostings to add flavor.

Grandpappy's Sour Cream Pound Cake

Every good Southern cook seems to have at least one recipe for pound cake. My grandfather was a pound cake fan; his week just wasn't complete without several servings of this rich cake.

1 cup unsalted butter
½ cup solid vegetable shortening
3 cups sugar
5 eggs
3 cups all-purpose flour
½ teaspoon baking soda
1 (8-ounce) container sour cream
¼ cup milk
1 teaspoon vanilla extract
Vanilla ice cream

Cream butter and shortening until light and fluffy with an electric mixer on low speed. Gradually add sugar, beating on medium speed until light and fluffy. Add eggs, one at a time, beating after each addition.

Preheat oven to 325° F.

Combine flour and soda, stirring well with a fork. Combine sour cream and milk. Add one-third of flour mixture to butter mixture with half of the sour cream mixture. Mix with an electric mixer on medium speed until blended. Add another third of the flour mixture and mix until blended. Add remaining flour mixture, remaining sour cream mixture, and vanilla. Mix until blended.

Pour batter into a heavily greased and floured 10-inch tube pan. Bake for 1 hour and 10 minutes to 1 hour and 15 minutes, or until a wooden pick inserted in center comes out clean. Cool in pan 10 minutes; turn out on a rack and cool completely. To serve, cut cake into slices, toast if desired, and top each slice with a scoop of ice cream.

Yield: one 10-inch tube cake.

Grandpappy's Sour Cream Pound Cake is an uncomplicated dessert with a rich, satisfying flavor. To dress it up, you can top the slices with ice cream, lemon sauce, chocolate sauce, or sliced strawberries.

Cider Sweet Apple Pie

You can cook any apple, but the Stay-man Winesap, the Red Rome, and the Granny Smith are some of the South's finest cooking apples. You can't miss the tart apple flavor in this pie because it also contains apple cider.

I have not come across any better apple pie than Cider Sweet Apple Pie. Tart fall apples are flavored with apple cider and surrounded with sugary pastry.

Double-Crust Pie Pastry, unbaked (recipe follows)
1 cup plus 2 tablespoons apple cider, plus a little extra
½ cup sugar
⅓ cup firmly packed brown sugar
7½ cups peeled, cored, and sliced cooking apples (8 to 9 apples)
2 tablespoons cornstarch
1 teaspoon ground cinnamon
1 tablespoon unsalted butter or margarine
2 teaspoons milk
1 teaspoon sugar for sprinkling on top of pie

Line a 9-inch pie plate with half of pastry and set aside.

Combine 1 cup apple cider, ½ cup sugar, and brown sugar in a large saucepan; bring to a boil. Add apples, and cook, uncovered, 8 minutes, or until apples are tender. Drain, reserving syrup. Add enough additional apple cider to syrup to measure 1⅓ cups liquid; return syrup mixture and apples to saucepan.

Preheat oven to 375° F.

Combine cornstarch and 2 tablespoons apple cider, stirring well; add to apple mixture. Stir in cinnamon; cook, stirring constantly, until thickened. Stir in butter. Spoon mixture into prepared pie plate. Cover with top pastry. Trim edges of pastry; seal and flute edges. Cut slits in top of pastry to allow steam to escape. Brush top of pastry lightly with milk. Sprinkle top of pastry with 1 teaspoon sugar. Bake for 45 to 50 minutes, shielding edges with foil if pastry browns too quickly.

Yield: 6 to 8 servings.

Double-Crust Pie Pastry

3 cups all-purpose flour
1 teaspoon salt
1 cup solid vegetable shortening
¾ cup cold half-and-half

Combine flour and salt in a bowl; cut in shortening with a pastry blender until mixture resembles coarse meal. Sprinkle cold half-and-half evenly over surface, stirring with a fork, until all dry ingredients are moistened. Shape dough into a ball; chill. Divide dough in half. Roll each half of dough to ⅛-inch thickness on a lightly floured surface and proceed with recipe.

Yield: pastry for one double-crust 9-inch pie.

Combine sugar, corn syrup, and ½ cup water in a large saucepan. Cook over medium-low heat, stirring constantly, until sugar dissolves. Cover and cook over medium heat 2 to 3 minutes to wash down sugar crystals from sides of pan. Add peanuts; cook, uncovered, stirring frequently, until mixture reaches the hard-crack stage (300° F. on a candy thermometer). Stir in butter, vanilla, soda, and salt.

Working quickly, pour mixture into a buttered jelly-roll pan; spread thinly. Let cool until firm; break into pieces. Store in airtight containers.

Yield: about 2 pounds.

Favorite Peanut Brittle

George Washington Carver would be pleased to taste this crunchy peanut brittle. It is a popular candy in south Georgia and south Alabama.

2 cups sugar
1 cup light corn syrup
½ cup water
2 cups raw or dry-roasted peanuts
2 tablespoons unsalted butter
1 teaspoon vanilla extract
1 teaspoon baking soda
¼ teaspoon salt

Favorite Peanut Brittle is made by cooking a mixture of sugar, corn syrup, water, and peanuts to the hard-crack stage; the hot mixture is spread into a buttered jelly-roll pan and cooled, then broken into pieces.

Apple Dumplings

During lean times, Southern cooks were known to be frugal. But an abundance of apples and leftover pastry scraps meant apple dumplings could be made—a real treat!

Dough:

    2 cups all-purpose flour
    2 teaspoons sugar
    ¼ teaspoon salt
    ½ cup solid vegetable shortening
    ¼ cup unsalted butter, softened
    1 egg, beaten
    ½ cup ice water

Filling:

    3 large, firm, tart cooking apples
    6 teaspoons unsalted butter or
        margarine
    3 teaspoons brown sugar
    1½ teaspoons ground cinnamon

Syrup:

    2 cups water
    1½ cups sugar
    3 tablespoons unsalted butter or
        margarine
    1 teaspoon ground cinnamon
    ½ teaspoon ground nutmeg

To make the dough, combine flour, sugar, and salt; cut in shortening and butter with a pastry blender until mixture resembles coarse meal. Combine egg and ice water; gradually add to flour mixture, stirring with a fork to make a soft dough. Cover and chill 1 hour.

On a floured surface, roll pastry out into a 21- x 14-inch rectangle; cut into six 7-inch squares. Peel and core apples; cut in half, crosswise. Place one apple half (cut side down) in center of each pastry square; dot each with 1 teaspoon butter. Sprinkle each with ½ teaspoon of the brown sugar and ¼ teaspoon of the cinnamon. Moisten edges of each dumpling with a little water; bring corners to center, pinching edges to seal. Use any extra pastry to make decorative leaf designs, if desired. Place the dumplings in a 13- x 9- x 2-inch baking dish; set aside.

Preheat the oven to 450° F.

To make the syrup: Combine the water, sugar, butter, cinnamon, and nutmeg in a medium saucepan; bring to a boil. Reduce heat and simmer, stirring frequently, until butter melts and sugar dissolves; set aside.

Bake dumplings, uncovered, for 10 minutes. Reduce heat to 350° and pour syrup mixture over the dumplings. Bake 30 minutes more, basting occasionally.

Yield: 6 servings.

For a real old-fashioned Southern dessert, try Apple Dumplings. Each apple half is wrapped in pastry and baked in a sweet syrup.

Elegant Pear Tart

When I was a child I thought pears were just for picking and eating. Later, I grew to appreciate this lovely pear tart.

Pastry:

  1½ cups all-purpose flour
  ½ teaspoon salt
  2 tablespoons sugar
  ¼ cup plus 2 tablespoons unsalted butter
  2 tablespoons solid vegetable shortening
  4 to 6 tablespoons cold milk

Filling:

  4 to 5 medium-size ripe pears
  3 tablespoons lemon juice
  3 tablespoons water
  2 tablespoons unsalted butter
  ¼ cup plus 2 tablespoons sugar
  3 egg yolks
  ¼ cup heavy cream
  1 tablespoon all-purpose flour
  1 teaspoon vanilla extract
  ¼ cup peach or apricot preserves

Combine flour, salt, and 2 tablespoons sugar in a small mixing bowl; cut in butter and shortening until mixture resembles coarse meal. Sprinkle milk evenly over surface, stirring with a fork, until all ingredients are moistened. Shape dough into a ball; chill.

Preheat oven to 375° F.

Roll dough out to fit a 10-inch tart

The pears in Elegant Pear Tart look pretty arranged in a fan shape. Each pear half is sliced and arranged in the pastry-lined tart pan before the sweet custard filling is added.

pan with removable sides. Prick pastry with a fork and bake for 15 minutes.

Peel and core pears. Combine lemon juice and water and dip pears in mixture; drain well. Cut pears in half lengthwise; cut each half into ½-inch-thick lengthwise slices. Arrange pears in tart pastry so that slices are overlapping. Dot with 2 tablespoons butter and sprinkle with 2 tablespoons sugar. Set aside.

Combine egg yolks and ¼ cup sugar; beat well. Add cream, 1 tablespoon flour, and vanilla; beat with a wire whisk until blended, then pour over pears. Bake at 375° F. for 25 to 30 minutes, or until set.

Cook preserves over medium heat, stirring constantly, just until melted, and brush over tart. Carefully remove sides of tart pan before serving.

Yield: 8 to 10 servings.

Perfect Pecan Pie

If there were a hall of fame for Southern food, pecan pie would certainly be featured. I'm not sure when or where the first pecan pie was made, but it's still a regional favorite.

Single-Crust Pie Pastry, unbaked
  (recipe follows)
1 cup dark corn syrup
½ cup sugar
½ cup firmly packed brown sugar
4 eggs, beaten
⅓ cup melted unsalted butter
1 teaspoon vanilla extract
Pinch of salt
1 cup pecan pieces

Line a 9-inch pie plate with pastry; trim and flute edges. Set aside.

Preheat oven to 325° F.

Combine corn syrup, sugar, and brown sugar, stirring well. Stir in eggs, melted butter, vanilla, and salt until well blended.

Sprinkle pecans in bottom of pastry-lined pie plate. Pour filling over pecans. Bake for 45 to 50 minutes, or until set, shielding edges with foil if pastry browns too quickly. Let cool before serving.

Yield: 6 to 8 servings.

Single-Crust Pie Pastry

1 ¼ cups all-purpose flour
¼ teaspoon salt
¼ cup plus 2 tablespoons solid
  vegetable shortening
4 to 5 tablespoons ice water

Combine flour and salt in a bowl; cut in shortening with a pastry blender until mixture resembles coarse meal. Sprinkle cold water, 1 tablespoon at a time, evenly over surface, stirring with a fork, until all dry ingredients are moistened. Shape dough into a ball; chill. Roll dough out to ⅛-inch thickness on a lightly floured surface and proceed with recipe.

Yield: pastry for one single-crust 9-inch pie.

There are two secrets to Perfect Pecan Pie: regular and *brown sugar, and pecan pieces rather than whole or chopped pecans.*

Fall Menus
Around the Harvest Table

One of the South's most famous fall rituals is the tailgate picnic. Football fans will "caravan" to games with family and longtime college friends, having packed the day's goodies in hampers and coolers.

Most people settle for casual fare—soups and stews, French bread or corn bread, cookies and brownies, beer and soft drinks. But some crowds with champagne taste have been known to spread tables with linen cloths and serve their feast on china and crystal. Even silver candelabra have graced stadium parking lots.

TAILGATE PICNIC

Football Brunswick Stew

Simple Pecan Meringues

Country Corn Sticks (page 32)

Famous Mississippi Mud Squares

After-School Oatmeal Cookies

Beer ♦ Soft Drinks

Football Brunswick Stew

Did it originate in Brunswick County, North Carolina; Brunswick County, Virginia; or Brunswick, Georgia? No one is exactly sure. Only this much is certain—the stew should contain chicken, potatoes, tomatoes, butter beans (limas), and corn, and it is infinitely better simmered in a large cast-iron kettle.

1 (1¾-pound) pork loin roast, trimmed
4 boneless, skinless chicken breast halves (about 1⅓ pounds)
1 cup chopped onion
1 cup chopped green bell pepper
1 to 2 tablespoons bacon drippings or vegetable oil
4 (14½-ounce) cans tomatoes, undrained and chopped
1 (8-ounce) can tomato sauce
¼ cup sugar
3 tablespoons Worcestershire sauce
2 tablespoons cider vinegar
2 cups water
2 tablespoons all-purpose flour
1 pound red potatoes, peeled and cubed
1 to 2 teaspoons hot sauce
1 teaspoon salt
½ teaspoon black pepper
¼ teaspoon ground turmeric
2 (16-ounce) cans whole-kernel corn, drained
1 (16-ounce) can lima beans, drained

An old cast-iron Dutch oven carries Football Brunswick Stew to the game. Bowls of the colorful soup are ladled up and served to the parents. The soup is thick with vegetables, chicken, pork roast, and tomatoes and is flavored with tangy vinegar and spicy hot sauce.

Combine pork roast and chicken breasts in a large kettle or Dutch oven; cover with water and bring to a boil. Cover, reduce heat, and simmer 1½ hours, or until meats are tender. Drain and cool meats completely. Chop into small pieces by hand or in food processor. Set aside.

Sauté onion and green pepper in bacon drippings in a large Dutch oven. Add chopped meats, tomatoes, tomato sauce, sugar, Worcestershire sauce, and vinegar.

Combine water and flour, stirring well. Stir flour mixture into meat mixture. Add potatoes, hot sauce, salt, pepper, and turmeric; stir well. Cover and cook over medium heat for 30 minutes or until potatoes are tender, stirring occasionally. Stir in corn and lima beans; cook 15 minutes more.

Yield: 10 to 12 servings.

Spread pecans on a heavily greased 15- x 10- x 1-inch jelly-roll pan. Bake for 25 to 30 minutes, stirring every 10 minutes. Cool completely; store in an airtight container.

Yield: 5 cups.

Simple Pecan Meringues

Pecan trees are abundant in south Georgia. While growing up there, I spent many an afternoon collecting and shelling these prized nuts. Here is my favorite way to eat them.

> 1 cup sugar
> 2 teaspoons ground cinnamon
> 2 teaspoons ground nutmeg
> ¼ teaspoon salt
> 1 egg white, at room temperature
> 2 tablespoons orange juice
> 5 cups pecan halves

Preheat oven to 300° F.

Combine sugar, cinnamon, nutmeg, and salt. In a large bowl, beat egg white and orange juice until foamy. Gradually add sugar mixture, beating until stiff peaks form. Fold in pecan halves.

Simple Pecan Meringues, offered from a glass pumpkin jar, make the perfect pre-game snack. The pecans are coated with sweet meringue and baked until crisp.

Famous Mississippi Mud Squares with Cocoa Frosting

Some folks claim that this recipe was named after the thick, rich mud found along the Mississippi River after a hard rain. Well, the idea of all that mud isn't appealing, but just the thought of these frosted brownies makes my mouth water.

1 cup unsalted butter
½ cup cocoa
2 cups sugar
1¼ cups all-purpose flour
1¼ cups chopped pecans
¼ teaspoon salt
4 eggs, beaten
1 teaspoon vanilla extract
2½ cups miniature marshmallows
Cocoa Frosting (recipe follows)

Melt butter in a small saucepan over medium heat; add cocoa, mixing well. Remove from heat and let cool.

Preheat oven to 350° F.

Combine sugar, flour, pecans, and salt in a large mixing bowl; stir well. Add eggs and vanilla, stir until blended. Stir in melted chocolate mixture.

Spoon batter into a lightly greased and floured 13- x 9- x 2-inch baking pan. Bake for 30 minutes, or until a wooden pick inserted in center comes out clean. Immediately sprinkle marsh-mallows over top of hot brownies. Spread Cocoa Frosting over marshmallows. Cool and cut into squares.

Yield: 15 servings.

Cocoa Frosting

½ cup unsalted butter
¼ cup plus 2 tablespoons milk
¼ cup plus 2 tablespoons cocoa
1 (16-ounce) package confectioners' sugar, sifted
1 teaspoon vanilla extract

Combine butter, milk, and cocoa in a small saucepan; cook over medium heat, stirring frequently, until butter melts and cocoa is well incorporated. Remove from heat and transfer to a medium mixing bowl. Add sugar and vanilla. Beat with an electric mixer on low speed until smooth.

Yield: 2 cups.

A tailgate dessert should be simple—something that can be grabbed and taken along if the game should start before the meal is complete. Famous Mississippi Mud Squares with Cocoa Frosting and After-School Oatmeal Cookies are popular with everyone. The thick cocoa-based brownies are filled with marshmallows and topped with a sweet cocoa frosting. The oatmeal cookies are unique; corn flakes make them extra crunchy, and brown sugar makes them extra sweet.

After-School Oatmeal Cookies

My son, Robert, loves being greeted in the afternoon with a couple of these crisp cookies and a glass of cold milk.

2 cups all-purpose flour
1 teaspoon baking powder
1 teaspoon baking soda
½ teaspoon salt
½ cup unsalted butter
½ cup solid vegetable shortening
1 cup sugar
¾ cup firmly packed brown sugar
2 eggs
1 teaspoon vanilla extract
2 cups quick-cooking oats, uncooked
1¾ cups corn flakes

Preheat oven to 325° F.

Combine flour, baking powder, soda, and salt; set aside.

Cream butter and shortening on low speed of an electric mixer until light and fluffy. Gradually add sugar and brown sugar, beating well at medium speed. Beat in eggs and vanilla. Add flour mixture, mixing well. Stir in oats and corn flakes.

Drop cookie dough by heaping table-spoonfuls onto lightly greased baking sheets. Bake for 12 to 15 minutes, or until golden. Cool slightly on baking sheets; remove to wire racks to cool completely.

Yield: about 3 dozen.

*O*n this important night, invite the neighbors to your house for a costume parade before trick-or-treating. It's a terrific way to become better acquainted, and a group will ensure a safe outing for everyone.

Before parting for the evening, invite your band of masqueraders back to the house for mugs of hot apple cider and bowls of chili. Top off this casual supper with slices of pumpkin pie or, for the children, peanut butter cookies. By evening's end, all the ghosts and goblins will be full, warm, and happy.

HALLOWEEN HARVEST SUPPER

Simple Pear Salad

Georgia Chili with Beans

Cheese Biscuits

Easy Sour Cream Pumpkin Pie

Classic Peanut Butter Cookies

Mulled Apple Cider

Simple Pear Salad

My mother has served this fruit salad for years, but because it is so simple, she has never bothered to write it down. I share it with you because the combination of tender greens, fruit, and cheese makes a first course or fruit side dish that is refreshing on any menu.

> 1 small head Bibb lettuce, leaves separated
> 4 purple kale leaves
> 2 very ripe fresh pears, peeled and halved, or 4 canned pear halves, drained
> 4 tablespoons mayonnaise
> 4 tablespoons (1 ounce) finely shredded sharp Cheddar cheese

Arrange lettuce and kale leaves. Top with pear halves. Place 1 tablespoon mayonnaise on top of each half. Sprinkle each half with 1 tablespoon cheese.

Yield: 4 servings.

Georgia Chili with Beans

Georgians aren't quite as fervent about their chili as Texans, but they do have strong feelings about the "real" way to make it: with ground beef or venison and lots of beans. Here is a version of this regional favorite that is absolutely the very best I've come across.

> 1 large onion, chopped
> 2 tablespoons vegetable oil
> 1½ pounds lean ground beef
> 2 (15-ounce) cans tomato sauce
> 2 (16-ounce) cans kidney beans, drained
> 1 (6-ounce) can tomato paste
> 1½ cups water
> 1 cup beer or water
> 3 tablespoons chili powder
> 1 teaspoon brown sugar
> 1 teaspoon cider vinegar
> ½ teaspoon salt
> ¼ teaspoon garlic powder
> ⅛ teaspoon cayenne pepper
> ⅛ teaspoon ground cumin
> 2 to 3 dashes hot sauce

I grew up eating Simple Pear Salad; it is wonderful with very ripe, fresh pears, but canned pear halves are also good. The pears make a pretty fall salad when arranged on purple kale and delicate Bibb lettuce.

Georgia Chili with Beans can be dressed up by adding toppings—corn chips, sour cream, and cheese. Toss a salad and add biscuits or corn bread, and the meal is ready.

Sauté onion in oil in a large Dutch oven until tender. Add ground beef; cook over medium heat until browned, stirring to crumble. Drain. Add remaining ingredients and simmer, uncovered, over low heat for 1 hour.

Yield: 8 to 10 servings.

Cheese Biscuits

Self-rising flour is preferred by many expert Southern biscuit bakers. This biscuit is made extra light with additional soda and buttermilk.

> *2 to 2¼ cups self-rising flour*
> *2 teaspoons sugar*
> *⅓ cup solid vegetable shortening*
> *1 cup (4 ounces) finely shredded Cheddar cheese*
> *1 cup buttermilk*
> *½ teaspoon baking soda*
> *3 to 4 tablespoons lightly salted butter or margarine, melted*

Combine flour and sugar; cut in shortening with a pastry blender until mixture resembles coarse meal. Stir in cheese.

Preheat oven to 425° F.

Combine buttermilk and soda; stir well. Add buttermilk mixture to flour mixture. Stir until dry ingredients are moistened. Turn dough out onto a floured surface, and knead lightly 1 to 2 minutes.

Roll dough out to ½-inch thickness; cut into rounds with a 2-inch biscuit cutter. Place on a lightly greased baking sheet and brush tops with a small amount of melted butter. Bake for 10 to 12 minutes, or until browned. Brush tops with melted butter again, if desired.

Yield: 20 biscuits.

Cheese Biscuits are perfect served alongside the chili, but they are also a tempting breakfast treat. In fact, I can think of several wonderful ways to enjoy these biscuits—split and filled with paper-thin slices of country ham, drenched with red-eye gravy, or spread with homemade strawberry preserves.

Easy Sour Cream Pumpkin Pie

Numerous recipes for pumpkin pie are tucked away in recipe boxes across the South. Most of the recipes are very similar, but this one is a little different because it uses sour cream rather than milk.

¾ cup sugar
¼ cup firmly packed brown sugar
½ teaspoon ground cinnamon
½ teaspoon ground nutmeg
¼ teaspoon ground ginger
⅛ teaspoon salt
2 cups mashed cooked pumpkin
1 (8-ounce) container sour cream
3 eggs, separated
Single-Crust Pie Pastry, unbaked
(page 42)

Combine sugar, brown sugar, cinnamon, nutmeg, ginger, and salt, stirring well. Add pumpkin and sour cream, stirring well.

Preheat oven to 400° F.

Beat egg yolks until thick and lemon-colored; stir into pumpkin mixture. Beat egg whites (at room temperature) until stiff peaks form; fold into pumpkin mixture.

Line a 9-inch pie plate with pastry; trim and flute edges. Pour in filling. Bake for 10 minutes. Reduce heat to 350°, and bake another 45 to 50 min-utes, or until set, shielding edges with foil if pastry browns too quickly.

Yield: 6 to 8 servings.

Classic Peanut Butter Cookies

My mother taught me how to make these cookies when I was in elementary school. Years later, I used this same recipe with my high school home economics students.

Simple and unadorned, Easy Sour Cream Pumpkin Pie is a traditional favorite with adults, while children are more eager to munch on Classic Peanut Butter Cookies.

¼ cup unsalted butter
¼ cup solid vegetable shortening
½ cup creamy peanut butter
½ cup sugar
½ cup firmly packed brown sugar
1 egg
1 teaspoon vanilla extract
1¼ cups all-purpose flour
½ teaspoon baking soda
½ teaspoon salt

Cream butter, shortening, and peanut butter on low speed of an electric mixer until smooth. Gradually add sugar and brown sugar, beating until light and fluffy. Add egg and vanilla, and beat well.

Preheat oven to 350° F.

Combine flour, soda, and salt; add to creamed mixture, mixing well. Cover and refrigerate dough 1 hour. Shape dough into 1-inch balls; place 2 inches apart on lightly greased baking sheets. Dip a fork in water and flatten cookies in a crisscross pattern to ¼-inch thickness. Bake for 10 to 12 minutes, or until lightly browned on edges. Let cool 2 minutes on baking sheets, then remove to wire racks and let cool completely.

Yield: 3 dozen.

Halloween night always seems to be rather cold and damp, so it is nice to have a mug of hot Mulled Apple Cider to sip. Although the recipe calls for a cup of rum or wine, a bit more ginger ale can be substituted to create a nonalcoholic drink.

Mulled Apple Cider

This cider creates a spicy aroma that drifts through the house, inviting everyone into the kitchen. I like to keep a pot of cider simmering on the stove all day on Thanksgiving.

1 medium-size orange
2 teaspoons whole cloves
1 gallon apple cider
3 cups ginger ale
1 cup light rum or white wine
⅔ cup red cinnamon candies
3 (3-inch) cinnamon sticks

Cut orange into 6 wedges; stud wedges with cloves. Set aside.

Combine cider, ginger ale, rum, and cinnamon candies in a Dutch oven; add orange wedges and cinnamon sticks. Cook over medium heat until candies are dissolved and mixture is thoroughly heated. Serve hot.

Yield: about 20 cups.

*T*he Southern kitchen is a hive of activity on Thanksgiving. The aroma of corn bread dressing flavored with turkey broth, sage, onion, and celery beckons us to the table. The recipe given here is a regional favorite, although some cooks prefer to use white bread instead of corn bread and may add pecans or sausage. The dressing might be stuffed inside the bird, baked separately, or shaped by hand into oval patties or pones and baked until brown and crisp.

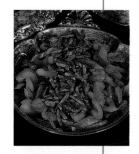

THANKSGIVING FEAST

Florida Hearts of Palm Salad with
Peanutty Dressing

Celery Amandine ♦ Oyster Casserole

Mary Emma's Turkey and Dressing
with Giblet Gravy

Glazed Orange Rolls

Orange-Glazed Beets

Festive Sweet Potato Casserole

Plantation Pumpkin Roll

Mama's Lane Cake
with Fruit Filling

Iced Tea

Florida Hearts of Palm Salad with Peanutty Dressing

I first sampled this unusual salad when visiting near McIntosh, Florida. The hearts of palm are actually the inner portion of the stem of the swamp cabbage palm tree, which is Florida's official state tree. Most of the hearts of palm we consume today come from South America, but Floridians still celebrate this delicacy at the annual Swamp Cabbage Festival in La Belle.

Dressing:

    ⅓ cup softened vanilla ice cream
    3 tablespoons mayonnaise
    3 tablespoons crunchy peanut butter
    2 tablespoons orange juice
    1 tablespoon milk or whipping cream

    2 heads Bibb lettuce, leaves separated
    1 (14-ounce) can hearts of palm,
        drained and sliced
    1 (11-ounce) can mandarin oranges,
        drained
    ½ cup drained pineapple chunks
    ½ cup sliced strawberries
    2 tablespoons dried currants or raisins
    2 teaspoons finely grated orange rind

To make the dressing, combine ice cream, mayonnaise, peanut butter, orange juice, and milk in a small bowl, stirring well. Cover and chill 1 to 2 hours.

Arrange lettuce leaves on six chilled salad plates. Arrange hearts of palm, orange slices, pineapple chunks, strawberries, and currants evenly over each salad. Drizzle chilled dressing mixture over each salad. Sprinkle with orange rind.

Yield: 6 servings.

Celery Amandine

Southerners love celery and often add it to soups, dressings, deviled eggs, salads, and pickles. Here it adds crunchy texture to a festive holiday side dish.

    2 tablespoons unsalted butter or
        margarine
    ½ cup slivered blanched almonds

Begin the Thanksgiving meal by sitting down to Florida Hearts of Palm Salad with Peanutty Dressing. This colorful fruit salad includes hearts of palm, pineapple chunks, mandarin oranges, strawberries, and raisins. The sweet dressing is made of ice cream, mayonnaise, peanut butter, and orange juice.

Golden almonds and pimiento add texture and color to Celery Amandine. The celery is coooked until crisp-tender and flavored with white wine.

4 cups diagonally sliced celery
1 tablespoon chopped onion
¼ teaspoon salt
⅛ teaspoon garlic powder
½ cup chicken broth
2 tablespoons diced pimiento
2 tablespoons dry white wine

Melt 1 tablespoon of the butter in a heavy saucepan over low heat. Add almonds and sauté until golden. Set aside.

Melt remaining tablespoon butter in a saucepan. Add celery, onion, salt, garlic powder, and chicken broth. Cover and cook over low heat for 8 to 10 minutes, or until celery is crisp-tender. Stir in pimiento and wine; cover and cook 2 minutes more. Sprinkle with almonds before serving.

Yield: 4 to 6 servings.

Oyster Casserole

Apalachicola, Florida, is famous for its oysters. Many cooks there serve oyster casserole on Thanksgiving.

2 (12-ounce) containers fresh oysters
¼ teaspoon salt
¼ teaspoon black pepper
⅛ teaspoon hot sauce
¼ cup chopped celery
¼ cup chopped green onion
¼ cup chopped green bell pepper
¼ cup minced fresh parsley
2 tablespoons lemon juice
2 teaspoons Worcestershire sauce
2 cups soda cracker crumbs
½ cup lightly salted butter, melted
½ cup half-and-half
Paprika

Preheat oven to 350° F.

Drain oysters and place half of them in a lightly greased shallow 2-quart baking dish; sprinkle with salt, pepper, and hot sauce. Top with half each of the vegetables, lemon juice, and Worcestershire sauce. Sprinkle with half the cracker crumbs. Drizzle with half the butter and half-and-half. Top with remaining oysters, vegetables, lemon juice, and Worcestershire sauce. Add remaining crumbs, butter, and half-and-half. Sprinkle paprika over all. Bake for 40 minutes, or until bubbly and lightly browned.

Yield: 6 servings.

Mary Emma's Turkey and Dressing with Giblet Gravy

Mary Emma Jefferson has been working her magic in my husband's family's kitchen in Decatur, Alabama, for over forty years. No Thanksgiving dinner is ever considered complete until a large platter of Mary Emma's turkey and dressing is placed in the center of the dining-room buffet.

> 1 (12- to 14-pound) turkey
> 1½ teaspoons salt
> ¼ cup unsalted butter or margarine, melted
> Turkey Dressing (recipe follows)
> Giblet Gravy (recipe follows)

Preheat oven to 325° F.

Remove giblets and neck from turkey; reserve for gravy. Rinse turkey with cold water; pat dry. Sprinkle salt over surface of turkey and inside cavity. Tie ends of legs to tail with string or tuck them under flap of skin around tail. Lift wing tips up and over back and tuck under turkey. Brush entire bird with melted butter.

Place turkey, breast side up, on a rack in a roasting pan. Insert a meat thermometer in the meaty part of a thigh. Roast for 4 to 5 hours, or until the meat thermometer registers 180° to 185°. Baste with pan drippings every hour. If turkey gets too brown, tent top with aluminum foil. After turkey has baked 3 hours, cut string or band of skin holding legs to tail. When done, let turkey stand 15 minutes before carving. Serve with Turkey Dressing and Giblet Gravy.

Yield: 14 to 16 servings.

Turkey Dressing

Corn Bread:

> 2 cups cornmeal
> ⅓ cup all-purpose flour
> 1 tablespoon sugar
> 1 teaspoon baking powder
> ¼ teaspoon baking soda
> ¼ teaspoon salt
> 2 cups buttermilk
> 3 eggs, beaten
> 1 tablespoon vegetable oil
> 1 tablespoon vegetable oil or bacon drippings

> 5 to 6 slices white bread, crumbled
> 1 onion, grated
> 2 stalks celery, finely chopped
> 3 to 4 cups chicken or turkey broth
> 1 teaspoon poultry seasoning
> ½ teaspoon white pepper
> ½ teaspoon rubbed sage
> ¼ teaspoon garlic powder
> ¼ teaspoon salt
> ¼ teaspoon black pepper

Combine cornmeal, flour, sugar, baking powder, soda, and salt in a large mixing bowl. Add buttermilk, eggs, and 1 tablespoon oil, mixing well.

Preheat oven to 450° F. Place 1 tablespoon oil or bacon drippings in a 10-inch cast-iron skillet. Place skillet in oven for 3 to 4 minutes. Tilt pan evenly to distribute oil or drippings; pour batter into pan and bake for 25 to 30 minutes. Cool; crumble corn bread into a large bowl. Add crumbled white bread. Set aside.

Combine onion and celery in a small saucepan. Add 3 tablespoons chicken broth. Cook over medium heat until vegetables are just tender; add to crumbled corn bread mixture. Stir in poultry seasoning, white pepper, sage, garlic powder, salt, and pepper. Add enough remaining broth for dressing mixture to hold together, adjusting for desired moistness (add up to 4 cups broth for a moist dressing; less for a drier dressing). Spoon mixture into a lightly greased 13- x 9- x 2-inch baking dish. Bake at 350° F. for 30 to 45 minutes, or until dressing is lightly browned and set.

Yield: 8 servings.

Giblet Gravy

Giblets and neck from 1 turkey
1 small onion, chopped
1 stalk celery, chopped
2 hard-cooked eggs, chopped
1 teaspoon salt
½ teaspoon black pepper
2 tablespoons cornstarch
¼ cup water

Cover giblets and neck with 3 cups water in a small saucepan. Bring to a boil; cover, reduce heat, and simmer 1 hour, or until giblets are tender. Drain, reserving broth, and discard turkey neck. Chop giblets and return to broth in saucepan. Add onion, celery, eggs, salt, and pepper. Bring to a boil; reduce heat, and simmer, uncovered, 30 to 45 minutes. Combine cornstarch and ¼ cup water, stirring well; stir into broth mixture. Bring to a boil; boil 1 minute. Serve hot.

Yield: 2½ cups.

Mary Emma's Turkey and Dressing with Giblet Gravy is the star of the buffet. Oranges, cranberries, kumquats, parsley, and fresh sage garnish the holiday platter. Any leftover turkey will be enjoyed at the evening meal in turkey sandwiches.

Glazed Orange Rolls

These sweet rolls practically melt in your mouth. They can be prepared in muffin pans, but I prefer them baked in square baking pans.

Dough:
  ¼ cup milk
  ¼ cup water
  ¼ cup unsalted butter or margarine
  ¼ cup solid vegetable shortening
  ¼ cup plus 2 tablespoons sugar
  ½ teaspoon salt
  1 package dry yeast
  ½ cup warm water (105° to 115° F.)
  1 egg
  1 egg yolk
  3 to 4 cups all-purpose flour

Filling:
  ½ cup unsalted butter or margarine, softened
  ½ cup sugar
  1 tablespoon grated orange rind

Glaze:
  2 cups sifted confectioners' sugar
  ¼ cup orange juice
  1 teaspoon vanilla extract

To make the dough, combine the milk, ¼ cup water, butter, shortening, sugar, and salt in a saucepan; heat over low heat until butter and shortening melt. Let cool until temperature reg-

isters 105° to 115° F. on a candy thermometer.

Dissolve yeast in ½ cup warm water in a large mixing bowl; let stand 5 minutes. Stir in melted shortening mixture, egg, and egg yolk. Gradually add 2 cups flour, beating with an electric mixer on medium speed until smooth. Stir in enough remaining flour to form a soft dough.

Turn dough out onto a lightly floured surface and knead until smooth and elastic (about 5 to 7 minutes). Place dough in a greased bowl, turning to grease top. Cover and let rise in a warm place (85° F.), free from drafts, 1 hour, or until doubled in bulk. Punch dough down and divide into 2 equal portions. Roll each portion out into a 12- x 8-inch rectangle.

To make the filling, combine ½ cup

Glazed Orange Rolls are a treat reserved for special occasions. If there are any leftover from the Thanksgiving meal, they can be reheated and enjoyed the next morning for breakfast.

butter, ½ cup sugar, and orange rind, stirring well. Spread half of this mixture over each portion of dough. Roll up each portion of dough jelly-roll fashion, beginning at long side. Pinch seams to seal. Cut each roll into 18 slices; place slices in paper-lined muffin pans or three 8-inch-square baking pans. Cover and let rise in a warm place, free from drafts, 1 hour.

Preheat oven to 350°.

Bake for 18 to 20 minutes, or until lightly browned.

To make the glaze, combine confectioners' sugar, orange juice, and vanilla, stirring well. Drizzle over warm rolls.

Yield: 3 dozen.

Orange-Glazed Beets look beautiful when offered from a cut-glass bowl and garnished with orange rind.

Orange-Glazed Beets

Fresh beets have more flavor, more color, and a crisper texture than canned beets. For best results, leave the roots and stems on the beets so as they cook, they will "bleed" less. Also, fresh beets are easier to peel after they have cooked and cooled.

3 pounds fresh beets
¼ cup unsalted butter or margarine
1 tablespoon plus 1 teaspoon sugar
1 tablespoon plus 1 teaspoon cider vinegar
1 tablespoon plus 1 teaspoon grated orange rind
¼ teaspoon salt
¾ cup orange juice

Leave root and 1 inch of stem on beets; scrub beets with a vegetable brush. Place beets in a large saucepan; add water to cover. Bring to a boil; cover, reduce heat, and simmer 35 to 40 minutes, or until tender. Drain; pour cold water over beets. Drain again. Trim off beet roots and stems; rub off skins. Dice beets and set aside.

Melt butter in a heavy saucepan over low heat; stir in sugar, vinegar, orange rind, salt, and juice. Cook over medium heat, stirring constantly, until smooth and thickened. Add beets; toss gently to coat. Cook 3 minutes, or just until heated through.

Yield: 6 servings.

Festive Sweet Potato Casserole

Ask a Southerner what he expects to have for Thanksgiving dinner, and he will certainly list sweet potato casserole. There are many similar versions of this recipe, and all of them are delicious.

6 medium-size sweet potatoes
¼ cup sugar
¼ cup firmly packed brown sugar
2 eggs, beaten
1 teaspoon vanilla extract
½ cup unsalted butter or margarine
⅓ cup milk
1 teaspoon ground cinnamon
½ teaspoon ground nutmeg
2 cups miniature marshmallows

Cook sweet potatoes in boiling water for 45 minutes to 1 hour, or until tender. Cool; peel and mash by hand.

Preheat oven to 350° F.

Combine sweet potatoes and the remaining ingredients, except marshmallows, in a bowl. Beat on medium speed of an electric mixer until smooth. Spoon mixture into a lightly greased 11- x 7- x 2-inch baking dish or a 2-quart casserole. Bake, uncovered, for 20 minutes. Sprinkle marshmallows over top of casserole; bake another 5 to 10 minutes, or until marshmallows are lightly browned.

Yield: 6 to 8 servings.

Plantation Pumpkin Roll

Creating something special out of something ordinary was the unique talent of many plantation cooks. This elegant dessert makes excellent use of the plentiful fall pumpkin crop.

3 eggs
¾ cup sugar
¼ cup firmly packed brown sugar
1 cup mashed cooked pumpkin
1 cup all-purpose flour
1 teaspoon baking powder
½ teaspoon salt
1 tablespoon ground cinnamon
½ teaspoon ground nutmeg
1 cup finely chopped pecans
2 to 3 tablespoons confectioners' sugar

Cream Cheese Filling:
1¼ cups confectioners' sugar
1 (8-ounce) package cream cheese, softened
¼ cup lightly salted butter, softened
1 teaspoon vanilla extract

Preheat oven to 375°.

Combine eggs, sugar, and brown sugar; beat on high speed of an electric mixer until smooth. Add pumpkin, mixing well. Combine flour, baking powder, salt, cinnamon, and nutmeg, stirring well; add to pumpkin mixture and mix until smooth. Pour batter into a greased and floured 15- x 10- x 1-inch jelly-roll pan, spreading evenly (batter will be thin). Sprinkle batter with pecans. Bake for 12 to 15 minutes, or until top of cake springs back when touched.

Sprinkle 2 tablespoons confectioners' sugar evenly on a tea towel. Loosen edges of cake, and carefully invert onto towel. Roll up cake in towel, beginning with short side. Cool cake completely.

Meanwhile, make the filling. Combine 1¼ cups confectioners' sugar, cream cheese, butter, and vanilla in a medium bowl. Beat with an electric mixer on medium speed until smooth.

Unroll cake, and spread with cream cheese filling to within ½ inch of edges. Carefully reroll cake without towel; chill before serving.

Yield: 8 to 10 servings.

Plantation Pumpkin Roll provides a memorable way to end the holiday feast. The swirled roll is studded with pecans that bake into the surface of the cake.

Mama's Lane Cake with Fruit Filling

Emma Rylander Lane, of Clayton, Alabama, developed the original Lane cake. My mother has served her version of this popular cake on special occasions for as long as I can remember. Many Southern cooks finish this cake by spreading the sides with fluffy white frosting. My mother likes to leave off the frosting; instead, she spreads the fruit filling between the layers and on the top of the cake.

1 cup unsalted butter or margarine, softened

2 cups sugar

3½ cups all-purpose flour

1 tablespoon baking powder

½ teaspoon salt

1 cup milk

1½ teaspoons vanilla extract

8 egg whites, stiffly beaten

Fruit Filling:

12 egg yolks

1⅔ cups sugar

1 cup lightly salted butter or margarine

1 tablespoon all-purpose flour

1½ cups finely chopped toasted pecans

1½ cups flaked coconut

1¼ cups raisins

⅔ cup finely chopped maraschino cherries

⅓ cup bourbon

In a large bowl, cream butter until light and fluffy with an electric mixer on low speed; gradually add sugar, beating well. Combine flour, baking powder, and salt and add to creamed mixture alternately with milk, beginning and ending with flour mixture. Mix well on medium speed after each addition. Mix in vanilla. Gently fold in egg whites.

Preheat oven to 350° F.

Pour batter into 3 greased and floured 9-inch round cake pans. Bake for 20 to 25 minutes, or until a wooden pick inserted in center comes out clean. Cool in pans 10 minutes; remove from pans and cool completely on wire racks.

While the cake is baking and cooling, make the filling. Combine egg yolks, sugar, butter, and flour in a 2-quart saucepan. Cook over medium heat, stirring constantly, 20 to 25 minutes, or until mixture thickens. Remove from heat and stir in pecans, coconut, raisins, cherries, and bourbon. Let cool completely, stirring occasionally, until thick enough to spread.

Spread filling between layers and on top of cake. If desired, filling may also be spread on sides of cake.

Yield: one 3-layer cake.

Mama's Lane Cake with Fruit Filling stands tall with three layers of delicate white cake. The fabulous fruit filling is a yolk-thickened mixture of pecans, coconut, raisins, cherries, and bourbon. There have been occasions when Mama made the fruit filling without the bourbon, but I think it was always missed.

Winter

Come in from the Cold

Winter brings a bite to the

air and draws us indoors by the fire.

Harsh cold marches across the hills and severs

the muted remnants of a season past. We flock toward

the heat, the lights, and family as we nest and

plan for warmer times.

Left: Found clustered high in the branches of trees, mistletoe is easily spotted once the trees have lost their leaves. In the late fall, mistletoe produces translucent white berries. The berries are carried by birds from one roosting spot to another, which helps explain why one tree may have many clusters of mistletoe while a nearby tree has none.

Old Man Winter expends most of his energy on Northern blizzards, but he still manages to blast Virginia, North Carolina, and Kentucky with enough snow and ice to justify a few Southern ski resorts. In Alabama, Mississippi, and Georgia, a few sleds hang idly on garage walls while their young owners scan the skies for heavy-hanging "snow clouds."

But with or without snow, darkness seems to

Center: The graceful trees and shrubs on the grounds of historic Longwood in Natchez, Mississippi, are adorned with thousands of tiny lights each Christmas. ♦ Right: A winter snow brings inconvenience, but it also brings beauty. These bright red berries look serene dressed with a light dusting of snow.

swallow more of each winter afternoon. The smell of woodsy smoke fills the cold air, as fires burn in Southern chimneys. Bringing in logs becomes a ritual that will last until spring. Families gather near their hearths to sip cider and reflect on the stark world outside, where only a few leaves cling to the trees and the grass is fading to brown.

This is the season when Southern kitchens

grow warm and fragrant with the baking of cakes, breads, cookies, and candy. The arrival of the Christmas season means preparing all sorts of delicious foods to be enjoyed by family and friends during the festive weeks of late December and early January. While cakes and breads cool, front doors, mailboxes, and mantels are draped and wrapped with greenery and cheerful ribbons. The scents of holly, pine, and juniper blend with those of cinnamon and citrus.

The days leading up to Christmas are punctuated by visits from friends and relatives. Hospitality prevails in the form of "open houses" when guests are invited to drop by to share a cup of eggnog or a light dinner.

On Christmas Day, children rise early to see toys left by Santa. After a few trips outdoors to try new bikes or skates, everyone gathers around the dining table for a midday Christmas dinner of baked ham or roast turkey, multiple vegetables and breads, ambrosia, fruitcake, and coconut cake.

After Christmas, New Year's Day ushers in more

cold weather and time spent around the table with friends. Cold evenings are perfect for sharing a pot of soup or stew, thick slices of bread, and wonderful desserts—chess pie, orange shortcakes, and gingerbread. Winter vegetables consist of turnips, broccoli, brussels sprouts, and carrots. Special holidays, like Valentine's Day, might be celebrated with a morning brunch of croissants spread with orange marmalade, a grits-and-sausage casserole, and sweet baked custards.

We often dread the cold and damp of winter, but when the season is over we are sometimes disappointed, for we miss the good food and the intimate time spent indoors with family and friends.

Above: Construction on Longwood, the largest octagonal house remaining in America, began in Natchez, Mississippi, in 1860. With the declaration of war in 1861, work on the home came to a halt and was never completed. The historic structure is maintained in its unfinished state by the Pilgrimage Garden Club and plays a vital role in the Christmas festivities planned each December. Adorned with thousands of tiny lights, Longwood looks like a grand carousel ready to twirl to a familiar holiday tune.

Above right and below: Stanton Hall, noted for its fine marble mantels and original gaslights, is often described as the most palatial house in Natchez. During the Christmas season, trees are decorated with Victorian lace ornaments; magnolia leaves and pinecones decorate the mantels, while poinsettias fill the fireplaces. Red and green apple trees stand guard on the sideboard in the dining room.

A Winter Welcome

We Southerners savor hospitality, particularly during the holiday season. So it's not surprising that each year, as soon as Thanksgiving is over, we turn our attention to decorating our homes for Christmas, inside and out.

Holiday decorations are not only fun and beautiful, they also send a message to friends and neighbors, telling them that they are welcome to stop by for a visit. This ritual probably began years ago when farmers were able to take some time off around Christmas, after the busy harvest season. The visiting gave farm wives a

Opposite: Holiday greenery climbs a lamppost and perches upon a mailbox, spreading a cheerful holiday message. Inset: Eva Royal, of Evening Shade, Arkansas, makes beautiful dried wreaths from pinecones, nuts, herbs, flowers, raspberry vines, and cayenne peppers. ✦ Above: Tours of the antebellum homes of Natchez take place several times a year. In the spring, the homes are lovely, with their old-fashioned gardens of azaleas and camellias. But the candlelight tours during December bring the sights, sounds, and scents of a Victorian Christmas to life. Trees are decorated to reflect the grandeur of their settings.

chance to sample one another's baked goods while the men compared notes about various crops and sampled a bit of muscadine wine or perhaps a little bourbon.

A street lined with gaily decorated mailboxes provides the first welcoming sign of Christmas. This is the neighbors' way of greeting us each time we leave the house. A spray of trimmed branches from the Christmas tree ornamented by a red or plaid bow pleases some people year after year. Others like to add a cluster of pinecones or holly leaves. Magnolia leaves, mixed with holly or nandina, also look beautiful perched on a mailbox and complemented with a stiff bow.

The front-door wreath is one of the most beloved and fussed-over Christmas customs. Those who live in traditional homes tie a generous red velvet bow on a fragrant balsam fir wreath and hang matching but smaller wreaths on the windows for a formal look. Ornamental fruits—pears, lemons, oranges, pomegranates, and

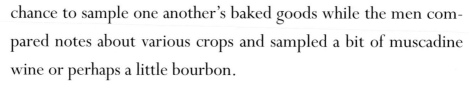

apples—and nuts are often added to the greenery for a rich display. Similar arrangements adorn porch lights on either side of the door, playing up the bounty of the season. Instead of a wreath, some homeowners might opt for a badge, or plaque, of evergreens and fruit.

Some homeowners dry herbs and flowers during the summer to use later in holiday wreaths. Others prefer traditional greenery tied with bright ribbons.

Above left: A garland of angels swags the staircase in the entry of this Birmingham home. Gold-edged ribbon ripples gracefully over the garland; wired ribbon, which holds its shape, can be purchased from most florists. ✦ *Above and right: It is exciting to see everyday mailboxes transformed into roadside greetings. Some of the boxes receive elaborate, creative arrangements, but most sport simple designs. The greenery is usually cut from yards and from trimmed branches of Christmas trees; it is nice to mix magnolia leaves with pine, fir, juniper, holly, or nandina. Pinecones, fruit, or brass hunting horns can also be worked into the designs. A cheerful waterproof bow of red velvet, red plaid, colored raffia, or metallic ribbon completes each design. To fashion a cluster for your mailbox, simply wire the greenery and bow to the nameplate or mailbox post.*

Wreaths made of dried flowers, grapevines, and herbs also have a tremendous following in the region.

Decorations do not stop at the front door. Inside, the Christmas tree in the living room is the center of attention. Parents and children will comb outdoor lots or tree farms to find the "perfect" one. Fireplace mantels and staircases are draped with pine garlands, ribbons, and bows. And the dining room and sideboard, festooned with magnolia leaves, baby's breath, apples, pineapples, and candlesticks, are ready for festive meals.

Church Fellowship

The church has always been the center of the South's soul. Even on cold winter Sunday mornings, when church bells peal, Southerners heed the call to worship. Many attend cathedral-like structures downtown in bustling cities or contemporary sanctuaries in the suburbs. But most of us continue to admire the beauty of serene country churches nestled along two-lane highways or dirt roads.

These modest single-room buildings may look alike at first glance. With their clean lines and stone or frame façades, they re-

Opposite and inset: Rural Southern churches, such as this one in Cades Cove, Tennessee, were usually built at crossroads or other spots convenient to several farms or plantations. The white-painted single-room buildings with rows of pews facing a central pulpit provided a place for preaching and a center for socializing with distant neighbors and friends. ♦ *Above: Yokena Presbyterian Church is located on Highway 61 in Mississippi, halfway between Vicksburg and Port Gibson. The small church, organized in 1884, was originally part of Hyland Plantation.*

Left: Historians believe this church in Mooresville, Alabama, was built in 1839 and was home to the Cumberland Presbyterian denomination. Over the years, the building has also housed Methodist and Baptist congregations. The steeple once had a large wooden hand pointing toward heaven, but it fell in the 1920s and has not been replaced. ♦ Below left: The Advent Episcopal Church was originally built in Lloyd, Florida, in the late 1800s but was later moved to its present location in Tallahassee. The tiny church seats about seventy-five people and is still being used.

call a simpler time. Some of the churches have no windows. Others have a few gothic windows and doors that arch sweetly. The structures often stand in grassy pastures or at crossroads where they were convenient to several farms or plantations.

Generations of Southerners have been baptized, married, and buried on the grounds of these churches. In the old days, farm life demanded backbreaking toil and offered little time for leisure. Gathering at church for Sunday worship and fellowship was welcomed as a social outlet. The visit of a church dignitary and other occasions prompted a dinner on the grounds. After the church service and sing, ladies would set baskets of food on long tables that stood permanently in a shady grove or a shedlike structure without walls. Following the blessing, everyone would circulate from table to table, sampling fried chicken, country ham, bread-and-butter pickles, green beans, sliced tomatoes and onions, squash casserole, field peas, corn on the cob, macaroni and cheese, marinated carrots, biscuits, corn bread, pies, and cobblers.

Sunday meals and church dinners gave farm wives a chance to

engage in some genteel competition among themselves. They would rise early on Saturday mornings to cook their favorite cakes. After the delicate layers had cooled, they were spread with a variety of rich frostings. Sometimes a sheet cake or a pound cake might win the ultimate compliment—the request by a neighbor for the recipe.

Many country churches still hold services from time to time. At others, descendants of members are invited to meet once a year on the church grounds for a day of worship, singing, and picnicking. Some families turn this event into an annual family reunion, giving everyone a chance to explore the past and discover more about the lives and be- liefs of ancestors who at- tended the churches.

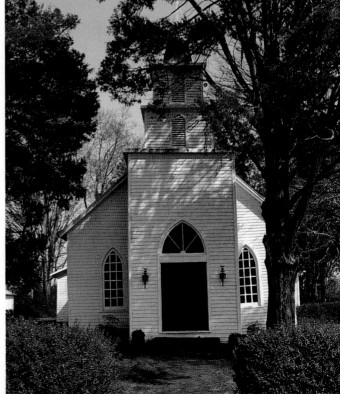

Above: This rural Tennessee church has three small windows on each side and a hand-pulled bell in the steeple. ♦ *Right: This pretty Methodist church is located in the small rural community of Belle Mina, Alabama. The church is named after Belle Mina plantation, which is situated in a grove of shade trees and giant boxwoods just down the road from the church.* ♦ *Above right: Situated near the Blue Ridge Parkway, this small stone church features beautiful stained-glass Gothic-style windows on each side.*

Winter Recipes
Savory Secrets

STEWS AND MAIN DISHES

In the old days, soups and stews helped Southern cooks stretch their budgets more than any other type of food. Cooks would take a little leftover roast beef, turkey, sausage, or chicken and simmer it into a flavorful broth that could be filled with vegetables, rice, or pasta.

In the winter, a big pot of soup might be put on the back burner early in the morning and left to simmer all day. At night, the soup would warm and nourish family members who had spent a cold day outside.

Modern Southern cooks still know the value of a hot bowl of soup, but for the sake of time, they must rely more and more on canned or convenience ingredients. Still, there is nothing to compare to a steaming bowl of stew made from fresh oysters or a thick soup brimming with vegetables and sausage.

Vegetable, Bean, and Sausage Soup

Following the annual fall butchering, Southern farm wives were challenged to come up with new and different ways to serve pork. One still-popular use of sausage is this flavorful vegetable and sausage soup.

> 1 pound bulk pork sausage
> 1 large onion, chopped
> ½ cup chopped green bell pepper
> ½ cup chopped celery
> 2 (16-ounce) cans kidney beans, drained
> 1 (28-ounce) can tomatoes, undrained and chopped
> 1 (8-ounce) can tomato sauce
> ½ teaspoon salt
> ¼ teaspoon garlic powder
> ¼ teaspoon dried thyme leaves
> ¼ teaspoon black pepper
> 1 cup peeled and diced red potato
> 1 large carrot, scraped and thinly sliced

Brown sausage in a large Dutch oven over high heat, stirring to crumble. Drain, reserving 1 tablespoon pan drippings; set sausage aside. Add onion, green pepper, and celery to drippings; sauté until tender. Add kidney beans, tomatoes, 1 quart water, tomato sauce, salt, garlic powder, thyme, and black pepper, stirring well. Bring to a boil over high heat; cover, reduce heat, and simmer 30 minutes. Add potato, carrot, and cooked sausage; cover and simmer 30 minutes or until vegetables are tender.

Yield: 8 to 10 servings.

Vegetable, Bean, and Sausage Soup looks dressy enough for company when served from this old Staffordshire pottery tureen.

Saturday Night Beef Stew

If you ask Southern cooks to tell you the difference between a soup and a stew, they will probably say that a stew is cooked in less liquid than a soup and is often thickened with flour or dumplings.

¼ cup plus 3 tablespoons all-purpose flour
2 teaspoons salt
1 teaspoon black pepper
2 pounds boneless beef chuck, cut into 1-inch cubes
3 tablespoons vegetable oil
1 small onion, sliced
1 teaspoon Worcestershire sauce
2 cloves garlic, minced
2 small bay leaves
4 medium potatoes, peeled and quartered
4 large carrots, scraped and cut into 2-inch pieces
4 small onions, cut into quarters
2 medium turnips, peeled and quartered
3 stalks celery, cut into 2-inch pieces

Combine ¼ cup of the flour, the salt, and the pepper in a bowl; dredge meat and shake off excess. Heat oil in a large soup kettle or Dutch oven and brown meat on all sides. Add sliced onion, Worcestershire sauce, garlic, bay leaves, and 5 cups water; stir, and bring mixture to a boil over high heat. Cover, reduce heat to low, and simmer 2 hours. Remove and discard bay leaves.

Add potatoes, carrots, quartered onion, turnips, and celery; cover and cook over low heat for 15 to 20 minutes, or until vegetables are tender.

Combine ¼ cup water and the remaining 3 tablespoons flour, stirring until smooth. Stir flour mixture into stew; cook until mixture is slightly thickened.

Yield: 8 servings.

Eastpoint Oyster Stew

Eastpoint, Florida, is a small coastal community between Tallahassee and Apalachicola that is dedicated to harvesting oysters. When I was a child we would often stop in Eastpoint and pick up several pints of oysters so we could make a stew similar to this one when we got home.

> ¼ cup lightly salted butter or
>   margarine
> 1 (10- or 12-ounce) container fresh
>   oysters, undrained
> ½ teaspoon salt
> ¼ teaspoon black pepper
> 1 quart half-and-half or milk
> ¼ cup dry white wine (optional)
> Paprika

Melt butter in a heavy saucepan; add oysters, oyster liquor, salt, pepper, and half-and-half. Cook over low heat, stirring until edges of oysters begin to curl. Stir in wine, if desired. Serve in soup bowls, sprinkled with paprika.

Yield: 4 to 6 servings.

Uptown Grits

This recipe dresses up regular grits with a mixture of bacon, green pepper, onion, celery, and tomatoes. The combination is addictive, so be prepared to offer second helpings.

> 6 slices bacon
> 1 clove garlic, minced
> 1 cup chopped green bell pepper
> ½ cup chopped onion
> ½ cup chopped celery
> 1 (16-ounce) can stewed tomatoes,
>   undrained
> 2 dashes hot sauce
> 1 teaspoon salt
> 1½ cups uncooked regular grits

Cook bacon in a large skillet until crisp; remove bacon, reserving 2 tablespoons drippings in skillet. Drain and crumble bacon; set aside.

Sauté garlic, green pepper, onion, and celery in drippings over medium heat until tender; stir in tomatoes and hot sauce. Bring mixture to a boil; reduce heat to low, and simmer 30 minutes, stirring occasionally. Set aside.

Meanwhile, combine 6 cups water and salt in a large saucepan; bring to a boil. Add grits. Cook over low heat, stirring occasionally, 10 to 20 minutes, or until grits become thick. Remove from heat; stir in tomato mixture and crumbled bacon. Serve immediately.

Yield: 6 to 8 servings.

Hoppin' John

According to Southern lore, everyone who eats this dish on New Year's Day will receive good luck throughout the year. So no matter how busy I might be, I always find time to cook these black-eyed peas.

2 cups dried black-eyed peas

¼ pound salt pork, cut into small cubes

⅔ cup chopped onion

½ cup chopped green bell pepper

⅓ cup chopped carrot

⅓ cup chopped celery

2½ cups water

1 cup regular long-grain rice, uncooked

1 bay leaf

½ teaspoon salt

¼ teaspoon dried hot red pepper flakes

¼ teaspoon dried thyme leaves

2 tablespoons chopped green onions

Sort and wash black-eyed peas; place in a Dutch oven. Add water until peas are covered by 2 inches. Let soak overnight.

Drain and rinse the black-eyed peas and return them to the Dutch oven; add enough water to barely cover peas. Add salt pork, onion, green pepper, carrot, and celery to peas. Cover and bring to a boil over high heat. Reduce heat to low and simmer 1½ to 2 hours, or until peas are tender and water has mostly cooked out.

Add 2½ cups water, rice, bay leaf, salt, red pepper flakes, and thyme to peas. Cover and cook over low heat for 20 to 30 minutes, or until rice is done, adding additional water if necessary. Sprinkle with green onions before serving.

Yield: 8 servings.

Hoppin' John is not very fancy, but it has plenty of flavor. My New Year's Day menu includes this traditional dish, served along with a skillet of corn bread.

DESSERTS

Every Southern family treasures its traditional cake, candy, pudding, and custard recipes, particularly those reserved for the family's Christmas dinner. There was a time when dining rooms or kitchens would have a special table, sideboard, or food safe just for displaying these fabulous holiday creations. The desserts would typically remain set up all through Christmas Day, and guests were free to return to the table or food safe as many times as they liked.

Carrot Cake with Cream Cheese Frosting

The use of carrots in cakes probably came about as an economy measure. Several cups of grated carrots add moisture to this large, luscious cake.

2½ cups finely grated carrots
2 cups all-purpose flour
1½ cups sugar
½ cup firmly packed brown sugar
2 teaspoons baking soda
1 teaspoon baking powder
½ teaspoon salt
2 teaspoons ground cinnamon
4 eggs, beaten
1⅓ cups vegetable oil
1⅓ teaspoons vanilla extract
Cream Cheese Frosting (recipe follows)

Preheat oven to 350° F.

Combine carrots, flour, sugar, brown sugar, soda, baking powder, salt, and cinnamon in a large mixing bowl. Stir well. Combine eggs, oil, and vanilla; stir into dry ingredients, mixing well. Pour batter into 3 greased and floured 9-inch round cake pans. Bake for 30 minutes, or until a wooden pick inserted in center comes out clean. Cool cake in pans 5 minutes; remove from pans and let cool completely on wire racks. Spread Cream Cheese Frosting between layers and on top of cake.

Yield: one 3-layer cake.

Cream Cheese Frosting

1 (8-ounce) package cream cheese
½ cup unsalted butter or margarine
1 (16-ounce) package confectioners' sugar
2 teaspoons vanilla extract
1 cup chopped pecans, toasted

Combine cream cheese and butter, beating with an electric mixer on medium speed until smooth. Add sugar and vanilla; beat until light and fluffy. Stir in pecans.

Yield: about 3½ cups.

Carrot cake with Cream Cheese Frosting is three moist, spicy cake layers, which are spread with a rich, nut-filled cream cheese frosting.

Granny Chason's Coconut Cake with White Fluffy Frosting

I have fond memories of my childhood visits with Granny Chason in Cairo, Georgia. Granny loved flowers, and was always tending what seemed like enormous beds of perennials, often sending me home with a huge bouquet. But more important, she always served a coconut cake, similar to this one, at the conclusion of our Sunday lunch.

¾ cup solid vegetable shortening

¼ cup unsalted butter

2 cups sugar

3 cups sifted cake flour

1 tablespoon baking powder

¾ teaspoon salt

1 cup milk

¼ cup water

1 teaspoon almond extract

½ teaspoon coconut extract

5 egg whites

White Fluffy Frosting (recipe follows)

2½ cups flaked coconut

Preheat oven to 350° F.

In a large bowl, cream shortening and butter until fluffy with an electric mixer on low speed. Gradually add sugar, beating on medium speed until light and fluffy. Sift together flour, baking powder, and salt; add to creamed mixture alternately with milk and ¼ cup water,

Coconut cake has always been a favorite with Southerners. During the holidays, this tall white cake takes an honored place on the dessert table, along with the ambrosia and eggnog. Granny Chason's Coconut Cake with White Fluffy Frosting was also a popular birthday cake at my house; I still request one every year.

beating well after each addition. Stir in almond and coconut extracts. Beat egg whites until stiff peaks form, and fold into batter.

Pour batter into 3 greased and floured 9-inch cake pans; bake for 20 to 25 minutes, or until a wooden pick inserted in center comes out clean. Cool in pans 10 minutes, then remove and cool completely on wire racks. Spread White Fluffy Frosting between layers and on top and sides of cake. Sprinkle with coconut.

Yield: one 3-layer cake.

White Fluffy Frosting

1¾ cups sugar

½ teaspoon cream of tartar

¼ teaspoon salt

½ cup plus 1 tablespoon hot water

5 egg whites

½ teaspoon coconut extract

½ teaspoon vanilla extract

Combine sugar, cream of tartar, salt, and hot water in a heavy saucepan. Cook over medium heat, stirring constantly, until sugar is dissolved and mixture becomes clear. Cook, without stirring, until syrup mixture reaches the soft-ball stage (240° F.) on a candy thermometer.

In a large bowl, beat egg whites with an electric mixer on high speed until soft peaks form; continue to beat, slowly adding syrup mixture. Add coconut and vanilla extracts. Continue beating until stiff peaks form and frosting is thick enough to spread.

Yield: about 8 cups.

Hot Curried Fruit

This is a recipe that has recurring popularity; every few years it is rediscovered and becomes the rage within that community of cooks. I think the spicy fruit combination is great served at brunch or as a dessert for a casual dinner.

Curry powder, brown sugar, and butter give ordinary canned fruit the sophisticated taste of Hot Curried Fruit. The spicy-sweet combination is the perfect addition to a brunch menu.

1 (29-ounce) can peach halves, drained

1 (29-ounce) can pear halves, drained

1 (20-ounce) can pineapple chunks, drained

1 (17-ounce) can apricot halves, drained

1 (4-ounce) jar maraschino cherries, drained

1 cup firmly packed brown sugar

½ cup unsalted butter or margarine, melted

1 tablespoon curry powder

Preheat oven to 350° F.

Combine peaches, pears, pineapple, apricots, and cherries in a 13- x 9- x 2-inch baking dish. Combine brown sugar, butter, and curry, stirring well; spoon over fruit. Cover and bake for 40 to 45 minutes, or until thoroughly heated.

Yield: 8 servings.

Orange Shortcakes

Here is Florida's wintertime equivalent to strawberry shortcake.

Shortcakes:

1 cup all-purpose flour
1 tablespoon sugar
1 teaspoon baking powder
¼ teaspoon salt
¼ cup plus 2 tablespoons unsalted butter
3 to 4 tablespoons milk

Orange Sauce:

7 large navel oranges
⅓ cup sugar
2 tablespoons unsalted butter or margarine
1½ teaspoons cornstarch
⅓ cup water
½ teaspoon lemon juice
½ teaspoon grated orange rind

Garnish:

Whipped cream

Preheat oven to 450° F.

To make the shortcakes, combine flour, 1 tablespoon sugar, baking powder, and salt in a bowl; cut in butter with a pastry blender until mixture resembles coarse meal. Gradually add enough milk to the mixture to form a soft dough, stirring just until dry ingredients are moistened. Turn dough out onto a lightly floured surface and knead lightly 4 or 5 times.

Roll dough out to ⅝-inch thickness; cut into four 3-inch circles. Place circles on lightly greased baking sheets. Bake for 8 to 10 minutes, or until lightly browned. Let cool completely on wire racks.

Peel and section oranges over a bowl to catch juice; reserve ⅓ cup juice.

Combine reserved juice and remaining ingredients in a medium saucepan. Cook over low heat, stirring constantly, until slightly thickened and bubbly. Remove from heat; stir in orange sections.

Split cooled shortcakes horizontally with a fork and gently pull apart. Place bottom half of each shortcake, cut side up, on each of 4 dessert plates; top with orange sauce. Cover with top half of each shortcake, cut side down. Spoon remaining orange sauce over each shortcake. Garnish each with a dollop of whipped cream.

Yield: 4 servings.

Opposite: Orange Shortcakes originated in central Florida, where there are acres and acres of orange groves. The flaky shortcakes are very much like biscuits.

Legacy Fruitcake will keep well for quite a long time if wrapped in brandy-soaked cheese-cloth and placed in a tightly covered container. More brandy must be added every seven days to keep the cheesecloth moistened.

Legacy Fruitcake

My father used to claim that the only fruitcake worth eating was a Jane Parker Fruitcake from the A & P or a Claxton Fruitcake from Claxton, Georgia. The recipe offered here rivals either of those cakes, and is crammed with nuts, raisins, and spices. You will want to make it a regular part of your holiday season.

1½ cups lightly salted butter, softened
¾ cup sugar
¾ cup firmly packed brown sugar
½ cup molasses
7 eggs, beaten
3½ cups all-purpose flour
3½ cups yellow, green, and red
    candied pineapple, chopped
2¾ cups red and green candied
    cherries, quartered
2 cups pecans, coarsely chopped and
    toasted
2 cups walnuts, coarsely chopped
1½ cups raisins
1 teaspoon ground cinnamon
½ teaspoon ground allspice
½ teaspoon ground cloves
¼ cup brandy
Additional brandy

Draw a circle with a 10-inch diameter on a piece of brown paper (not recycled paper), using a large, deep tube pan as a guide. Cut out circle; set tube pan insert in center, and draw around inside tube. Cut out smaller circle. Grease one side of paper, and set aside. Heavily grease and flour a deep 10-inch tube pan; set aside.

In a large bowl, cream butter until fluffy with an electric mixer on low speed. Gradually add sugar and brown sugar, beating well on medium speed. Add molasses, beating well. Alternately add beaten eggs and 3 cups of the flour to creamed mixture, beating well after each addition.

Combine candied pineapple, cherries, pecans, walnuts, and raisins in a large bowl; sprinkle with the remaining ½ cup flour, cinnamon, allspice, and cloves, stirring to coat well. Stir mixture into batter.

Spoon batter into prepared pan, pressing firmly, if necessary. Cover pan with the 10-inch paper circle, greased side down. Bake for 4 hours, or until a wooden pick comes out clean. Remove from oven. Discard paper circle. Carefully loosen cake from pan and invert onto a wire rack. Pour ¼ cup brandy evenly over cake. Cook cake completely. Wrap cake in brandy-soaked cheesecloth, and store in an airtight place for 3 weeks. Continue to pour a small amount of brandy over cake every 7 days.

Yield: one 10-inch cake.

Buttermilk Pralines

When I was about seven years old, my uncle brought me some pralines from New Orleans. I found the flat pecan patties to be irresistible, and I still do.

1¾ cups sugar
¼ cup firmly packed brown sugar
1 teaspoon baking soda
1 cup buttermilk
1 teaspoon vanilla extract
1 tablespoon lightly salted butter
2 cups pecan halves

Butter a sheet of wax paper and set aside. Butter the sides of a Dutch oven.

Combine sugar, brown sugar, baking soda, and buttermilk in a Dutch oven. Slowly bring mixture to a boil over low heat, stirring constantly, until sugar dissolves. Cover, increase heat to medium, and cook 2 to 3 minutes to wash down sugar crystals from sides of pan. Uncover and continue cooking, stirring occasionally, until mixture reaches soft-ball stage (234° F.) on a candy thermometer. Remove from heat; add vanilla, butter, and pecans. Beat vigorously with a wooden spoon until mixture just becomes glossy and begins to thicken. Working rapidly, drop mixture by heaping tablespoonfuls onto buttered wax paper; let stand until cool. Remove and store in an airtight container.

Yield: about 2 dozen.

French Quarter Bread Pudding with Lemon Rum Sauce

Bread pudding is a favorite in New Orleans. The secret is to use stale French bread and allow it to sit long enough to soak up the milk and egg mixture evenly.

4 eggs
1 cup sugar
1½ teaspoons vanilla extract
1½ teaspoons ground cinnamon
1 teaspoon ground nutmeg
½ cup unsalted butter, melted
2 cups milk
⅓ cup raisins
½ cup chopped pecans, toasted
5 cups stale French bread cubes
   (1-inch)
Lemon Rum Sauce (recipe follows)

In a large bowl, beat eggs with an electric mixer on high speed until thick and lemon-colored. Add sugar, vanilla, cinnamon, nutmeg, and butter; beat at high speed until blended. Stir in milk, raisins, and pecans.

Place bread cubes in a lightly greased 8-inch-square baking pan. Pour egg mixture over bread, stirring until all bread is soaked. Let stand at room temperature about 30 minutes, lightly mashing bread down in egg mixture occasionally.

Preheat oven to 300° F.

French Quarter Bread Pudding with Lemon Rum Sauce is a fairly simple, delicious baked dessert made with cubes of French bread that have been saturated with a mixture of eggs, milk, sugar, and butter. The baked pudding is best cut into squares and topped with the sweet sauce.

Bake for 40 minutes. Increase oven temperature to 425° and bake 10 minutes more, or until pudding is browned and puffy.

To serve, cut pudding into squares. Place each square in a dish and top with Lemon Rum Sauce.

Yield: 4 to 6 servings.

Lemon Rum Sauce

½ *cup unsalted butter*
1 cup sifted confectioners' sugar
1 tablespoon rum
1 egg, beaten
1 tablespoon lemon juice
1 teaspoon grated lemon rind

Place butter in top of a double boiler; bring water underneath to a boil. Reduce heat to low; cook until butter melts. Add sugar and rum, stirring until sugar dissolves.

Gradually stir about one fourth of hot mixture into beaten egg; add egg mixture to remaining hot mixture in pan, stirring constantly. Cook, stirring constantly, 5 minutes, or until sauce thickens. Remove from heat; stir in lemon juice and lemon rind.

Yield: 1 cup.

Winter Menus
Festive Celebrations

The hectic pace of modern times can eclipse the gracious lifestyle our region's ancestors held dear. But during Christmas, legendary Southern hospitality reemerges, and we entertain with a round of parties. One of the most popular is the open house. If the party is an afternoon gathering, the menu will almost certainly include drinks and dainty appetizers. But in the evening, hostesses like to provide a bit more substantial fare—a buffet that includes meatballs and small servings of red beans and rice.

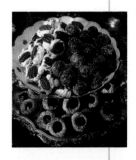

CHRISTMAS OPEN HOUSE

Aunt Alma's Eggnog

Party Cheese Cannonball

Holiday Cocktail Meatballs

Red Beans and Rice

French Bread

Gingerbread Men

Thumbprint Cookies

Bourbon Balls ◆ Divinity

Aunt Alma's Eggnog

My Aunt Alma always maintained that properly made eggnog should be thick enough to eat with a spoon. The recipe below was one that she enjoyed each Christmas. I have made one slight alteration to her recipe, however—I've cooked the custard mixture, because we have all been advised to avoid eating raw eggs.

> 6 large eggs
> ½ cup sugar
> 2 cups half-and-half
> 2 cups milk
> ½ cup brandy
> ¼ cup light rum
> 1 teaspoon vanilla extract
> 2 cups heavy cream
> 2 tablespoons sugar

Garnish:
> *Freshly grated nutmeg*

Beat eggs with an electric mixer on medium speed until thick and lemon-colored; gradually add ½ cup sugar, beating well.

Place half-and-half and milk in a large saucepan over medium-low heat; cook until thoroughly heated (about 150° F. on a candy thermometer) but not boiling. Gradually add the hot milk mixture to the egg mixture, stirring with a wire whisk. Transfer the mixture back to the large saucepan and cook over medium-low heat, stirring constantly with a wire whisk, until mixture reaches 165° F. on a candy thermometer. Remove from heat and let cool. Stir in brandy, rum, and vanilla with a wire whisk. Cover and chill thoroughly.

Just before serving, beat heavy cream and 2 tablespoons sugar in a large bowl until soft peaks form. Pour the chilled eggnog mixture into a punch bowl. Fold the whipped cream into the eggnog mixture gently but thoroughly. Garnish each serving with freshly grated nutmeg. Serve immediately.

Yield: 8 cups.

Party Cheese Cannonball

This round, firm cheese ball appears quite often at Christmas open houses and dinner parties in the South. Although the ingredients may vary slightly from hostess to hostess, this tried-and-true appetizer is always a hit.

Party Cheese Cannonball is made with cream cheese, Cheddar cheese, olives, onion, and green pepper; a little hot sauce and cayenne give the spreadable mixture just a bit of a bite.

2 (8-ounce) packages cream cheese, softened
2 cups (8 ounces) shredded sharp Cheddar cheese
3 tablespoons finely chopped pimiento-stuffed olives
2 tablespoons finely chopped pimiento, drained
1 tablespoon grated onion
1 tablespoon finely minced green bell pepper
1 tablespoon Worcestershire sauce
2 teaspoons lemon juice
½ teaspoon hot sauce
¼ teaspoon cayenne pepper
¼ teaspoon salt
1½ cups finely chopped pecans, toasted

Combine cream cheese and Cheddar cheese in a large mixing bowl; beat with an electric mixer on medium speed until blended. Stir in olives, pimiento, onion, green pepper, Worcestershire sauce, lemon juice, hot sauce, cayenne, and salt. Shape mixture into a ball, and roll the ball in chopped pecans. Wrap in plastic wrap and chill overnight. Serve at room temperature.

Yield: one 5-inch cheese ball (3 cups).

Holiday guests will appreciate being greeted with a cup of Aunt Alma's Eggnog. The thick, creamy beverage should be sprinkled with nutmeg before it is served.

Holiday Cocktail Meatballs

I've always had a passion for these sweet, tangy meatballs. They make a fine presentation when served from a silver chafing dish. I have seen them served on numerous occasions, from formal weddings to relaxed family holiday gatherings.

1 ½ pounds ground beef
½ cup fine dry bread crumbs
⅓ cup minced onion
¼ cup milk
1 egg, beaten
1 tablespoon minced fresh parsley
1 tablespoon soy sauce
½ teaspoon salt
⅛ teaspoon garlic powder
⅛ teaspoon black pepper
3 tablespoons vegetable oil
1 (16-ounce) jar grape jelly
1 (12-ounce) jar chili sauce
1 tablespoon brown sugar
2 teaspoons lemon juice

Combine beef, bread crumbs, onion, milk, egg, parsley, soy sauce, salt, garlic powder, and pepper in a large mixing bowl; shape into 1-inch meatballs. Cook in oil over medium heat for 10 to 15 minutes or until browned. Drain on paper towels.

Combine jelly, chili sauce, brown sugar, and lemon juice in a medium

Have the wooden picks handy when you serve Holiday Cocktail Meatballs, for guests will be eager to try this sweetly sauced appetizer.

saucepan; stir well. Add meatballs; simmer 10 minutes. Serve in a chafing dish with wooden toothpicks.

Yield: 5 dozen.

Red Beans and Rice

Folks from New Orleans serve red beans and rice quite often. You can control the spicy hot flavor of this recipe by varying the amount of hot sauce that is added.

1 pound dried red kidney beans
1 to 1½ pounds smoked meaty ham
    hocks
2 cups chopped onion
2 cups chopped celery
2 cups chopped green bell pepper
¼ cup chopped fresh parsley
1 (8-ounce) can tomato sauce
3 bay leaves
1 teaspoon white pepper
1 teaspoon dried thyme leaves
1 teaspoon garlic powder
1 teaspoon dried oregano leaves
1 teaspoon cayenne pepper
½ teaspoon salt
½ teaspoon black pepper
½ to 1 teaspoon hot sauce
1 pound andouille or other smoked
    sausage, cut into ½-inch pieces
Hot cooked rice

Sort and wash beans; place in a soup kettle or large Dutch oven. Add water until beans are covered by 2 inches; let soak overnight. The next day, drain and rinse beans. Add enough water to barely cover beans. Add rest of ingredients except sausage and rice; bring to a boil over high heat. Cover tightly, reduce heat, and simmer 1 hour and 45 minutes.

Remove ham hocks, and set aside. Add sausage to mixture. Cook, uncovered, over low heat for 40 minutes, stirring occasionally. Remove and discard bay leaves. Return meaty portion of ham hocks to bean mixture; stir well. Cook, uncovered, until thoroughly heated and mixture is desired thickness. Serve bean mixture over rice.

Yield: 6 servings.

Red Beans and Rice makes a spicy addition to holiday menus. When serving a crowd, ladle the flavorful mixture into small bowls or cups and have plenty of spoons on hand.

French Bread

This bread may not have originated in the South, but it has become extremely popular, especially in Louisiana, where it is crucial in the making of *pain perdu*, otherwise known as French toast.

> *3 packages active dry yeast*
> *1 teaspoon sugar*
> *2½ cups warm water (105° to*
>   *115° F.)*
> *8 to 8½ cups white bread flour*
> *1 tablespoon plus 1 teaspoon salt*

Dissolve yeast and sugar in warm water; let stand 5 minutes. Stir gently to make sure yeast is dissolved.

Sift 8 cups flour with the salt into a large bowl, stirring gently to combine; add yeast mixture, mixing well to make a soft dough.

Turn dough out onto a floured surface, and knead 5 to 10 minutes, or until smooth and elastic. Sprinkle dough generously with flour so dough will not form a crust. Cover dough with plastic wrap and let rise in a warm place (85° F.), free from drafts, for 2 to 3 hours.

Sprinkle large baking sheets with flour; set aside. Punch dough down; knead dough quickly, then divide into 4 equal portions. Shape each portion into a long roll, about 15 inches long. Place rolls on floured baking sheets. Cover with plastic wrap and let rise in a warm place (85° F.) for 30 minutes.

Preheat oven to 425° F.

Gently cut ¼-inch-deep diagonal slashes in loaves with a razor. Spray loaves lightly with water. Bake for 15 minutes. Reduce heat to 350° F. and bake 15 to 20 minutes, or until loaves are golden and sound hollow when tapped.

Yield: 4 loaves.

Sliced French Bread goes hand in hand with Red Beans and Rice. If you are short on time, the bread can be purchased from the bakery.

Gingerbread Men

These cookies contain two ingredients that were staples in early Southern pantries—ginger and molasses. I like to decorate the cookies with raisins and cinnamon candies.

½ cup solid vegetable shortening
½ cup firmly packed brown sugar
½ cup molasses
1 egg
3½ cups all-purpose flour
1 teaspoon baking powder
½ teaspoon baking soda
¼ teaspoon salt
1 teaspoon ground ginger
½ teaspoon ground cinnamon
½ teaspoon ground cloves
½ cup buttermilk

Garnish:
Raisins and cinnamon candies

In a large bowl, cream shortening with an electric mixer on low speed. Gradually add sugar, beating at medium speed until light and fluffy. Add molasses and egg and beat well. Combine flour, baking powder, soda, salt, and spices, stirring well. Add to creamed mixture alternately with buttermilk, beginning and ending with flour mixture, stirring well after each addition. Shape dough into a ball; cover and refrigerate at least 2 hours.

Preheat oven to 375° F.

Roll dough out onto a lightly floured surface to ¼-inch thickness; cut with a 3- to 4-inch gingerbread-man cutter. Place on lightly greased baking sheets. Press raisins into dough for eyes, nose, and mouth. Use cinnamon candies for buttons. Bake for 10 minutes. Let cool slightly on baking sheets. Cool on wire racks.

Yield: 2 to 3 dozen.

Youngsters will be thrilled when they spot a group of cellophane-wrapped Gingerbread Men. The cookies are given to guests to take home and enjoy after the party.

Thumbprint Cookies

These cookies are filled with strawberry preserves, but they would be equally tempting filled with your favorite jam or jelly.

> *1 cup unsalted butter or margarine,*
> *   softened*
> *¾ cup sugar*
> *2 egg yolks*
> *1 teaspoon vanilla extract*
> *2⅓ cups all-purpose flour*
> *¼ teaspoon salt*
> *Confectioners' sugar*
> *Strawberry preserves*

Cream butter with an electric mixer on low speed; gradually add sugar, beating on medium speed until light and fluffy. Add egg yolks, beating well. Stir in vanilla.

Combine flour and salt, stirring well; add to creamed mixture, mixing well. Cover and refrigerate dough 2 hours.

Preheat oven to 300° F.

Roll dough into 1-inch balls; place balls about 2 inches apart on ungreased baking sheets. Press thumb in each ball of dough, leaving an indentation. Bake for 20 to 25 minutes, or until lightly browned around edges. Cool cookies on wire racks. Sprinkle cookies with powdered sugar. Place ¼ teaspoon strawberry preserves in each cookie indentation.

Yield: 3½ dozen.

Bourbon Balls

Bourbon balls are a simple, no-cook holiday confection. They are popular with everyone, and a particular favorite of reluctant teetotalers, who can nibble on these without being reprimanded.

> *1¼ cups finely crushed vanilla wafer*
> *   crumbs*
> *1¼ cups sifted confectioners' sugar*
> *1 cup finely chopped pecans*
> *2 tablespoons cocoa*
> *2 tablespoons light corn syrup*
> *3 to 4 tablespoons bourbon*
> *Sugar*

Combine vanilla wafer crumbs, confectioners' sugar, pecans, and cocoa; mix well. Combine corn syrup and bourbon; mix well and stir into crumb mixture. Cover and refrigerate mixture for at least 30 minutes. Shape into 1-inch balls and roll each in sugar. Store in an airtight container.

Yield: about 3 dozen.

Divinity, Bourbon Balls, and Thumbprint Cookies look beautiful presented from a tiered dessert tray. Rolled in sugar, the Bourbon Balls are just as inviting as the pecan-topped candy and the strawberry-filled cookies.

Divinity

As the name implies, this traditional candy tastes absolutely divine. Be sure to prepare these rich white mounds on a dry, clear day. If exposed to humidity, the candy may turn out grainy and sticky.

2¾ cups sugar
½ cup hot water
½ cup light corn syrup
2 egg whites
Pinch of salt
1 teaspoon vanilla extract
2½ to 3 dozen pecan halves, toasted

Combine sugar, water, and corn syrup in a 3-quart saucepan; cook over low heat, stirring constantly, until sugar dissolves. Cover, raise heat to medium, and cook for 2 to 3 minutes more to wash down sugar crystals from sides of pan. Uncover and continue cooking over medium heat, without stirring, until mixture reaches hard-ball stage (260° F.) on a candy thermometer. Remove from heat.

Place egg whites in a large mixing bowl and beat with an electric mixer on high speed until stiff peaks form.

Pour hot sugar syrup in a thin stream over beaten egg whites while beating constantly at high speed. Add salt and vanilla and continue beating until mixture becomes firm enough to hold its shape when dropped by teaspoonfuls onto wax paper. Gently press a pecan half onto the top of each piece of candy. Let cool. Store in an airtight container.

Yield: about 1½ pounds.

This menu provides a wonderful way to reciprocate holiday invitations and share a little laughter with friends. Chutney, so adored by Southerners, makes an irresistible spread when paired with cream cheese. And black-eyed peas are transformed into a snappy appetizer, a definite hit with guests, since a helping of this Southern staple is supposed to ensure good luck all year long. The pork roast looks pretty surrounded by glazed brussels sprouts. By the time the midnight countdown starts, your guests will have eaten their share of chess pie or gingerbread cake with lemon sauce.

NEW YEAR'S EVE CELEBRATION

Carolina Chutney Log

Confederate Caviar

Citrus-Avocado Salad
with Honey Dressing

Apple-Baked Pork Roast

Pecan-Glazed Brussels Sprouts

Mary Emma's Ice Box Rolls

Pantry Chess Pie

Gingerbread Cake with Lemon Sauce

Champagne ♦ Coffee

Carolina Chutney Log

Chutney is a popular Southern condiment. It is delicious in this chutney log when spread over crackers.

1 (8-ounce) package cream cheese, softened
1 (3-ounce) package cream cheese, softened
3 tablespoons sour cream
2 teaspoons curry powder
¾ cup chopped roasted peanuts
½ cup chutney, finely chopped
¼ cup chopped green onions
3 tablespoons golden raisins, coarsely chopped
½ cup flaked coconut, toasted

Combine cream cheese, sour cream, and curry powder in a large mixing bowl; blend until smooth. Stir in peanuts, chutney, green onions, and raisins. Cover and chill 1 hour. Shape mixture into one large log or two smaller logs. Wrap in plastic wrap and chill overnight. Roll log in toasted coconut before serving.

Yield: one large or two small logs.

Confederate Caviar

Black-eyed peas have been a basic ingredient in Southern households since long before the War Between the States, but this tasty appetizer gives them new respect.

3 (15-ounce) cans black-eyed peas, drained
¼ cup chopped green onions
¼ cup chopped green bell pepper
2 tablespoons diced pimiento
1 jalapeño pepper, seeded and minced

Vinaigrette:
¾ cup vegetable oil
¼ cup red wine vinegar
⅛ teaspoon garlic powder
⅛ teaspoon salt
⅛ teaspoon black pepper
4 dashes hot sauce
Tortilla chips for serving

Combine black-eyed peas, green onions, green pepper, pimiento, and jalapeño pepper in a large bowl, stirring well. Set aside.

Whisk together the remaining ingredients, except tortilla chips, to make a vinaigrette. Pour over peas; toss gently. Cover and marinate in refrigerator overnight. Serve with tortilla chips.

Yield: 6½ cups.

Citrus-Avocado Salad with Honey Dressing

During the winter months, Florida is the largest producer of oranges, grapefruits, and avocados in the country. Here is one of the best ways I know to enjoy all three at one time.

4 cups torn spinach leaves
4 cups torn romaine lettuce
1 cup torn iceberg lettuce
2 oranges, peeled and sectioned, membranes removed
1 grapefruit, peeled and sectioned, membranes removed
1 avocado, peeled and sliced
1 tablespoon lemon juice
1 small onion, sliced and separated into rings
½ cup sliced celery
½ cup coarsely chopped pecans, toasted

Honey Dressing:
⅓ cup sugar
2½ tablespoons lemon juice
2½ tablespoons honey
2 tablespoons cider vinegar
½ teaspoon dry mustard
½ teaspoon paprika
¼ teaspoon salt
⅛ teaspoon celery seeds
½ cup vegetable oil

Combine spinach, romaine, and iceberg lettuce in a large bowl; toss gently. Arrange orange sections and grapefruit sections over salad greens. Toss avocado slices gently with lemon juice; discard lemon juice. Arrange avocado, onion, and celery over salad. Sprinkle with pecans.

Make the dressing by combining all the ingredients, except the oil, in container of an electric blender; process until smooth. While blender is running, slowly pour in oil; continue to process a few seconds until blended. Serve dressing over salad.

Yield: 6 to 8 servings.

Citrus-Avocado Salad with Honey Dressing is a wonderful way to begin a winter meal. Juicy grapefruits and oranges and buttery avocados are plentiful during this season.

Apple-Baked Pork Roast

This pork roast is an elegant dish that is easy to prepare and perfect for company.

> 1 (4- to 5-pound) rolled boneless pork
>   loin roast
> 1 teaspoon dried whole rosemary,
>   crushed
> ½ teaspoon salt
> ½ teaspoon garlic powder
> 3 tablespoons apple jelly
> 2 tablespoons honey mustard
> 2 tablespoons apple juice
> 1 tablespoon brown sugar

Preheat oven to 325° F.

Place roast, fat side up, on a rack in a shallow roasting pan. Rub roast with rosemary; sprinkle with salt and garlic powder. Insert meat thermometer, making sure it does not touch fat. Bake for 1 hour and 45 minutes. Remove roast from oven; leave oven on.

Combine apple jelly, honey mustard, apple juice, and brown sugar, stirring well. Brush roast with jelly mixture. Continue to bake at 325° F. for 15 to 30 minutes, or until thermometer registers 160° F.

Yield: 8 to 10 servings.

Apple-Baked Pork Roast is rubbed with rosemary and brushed with a mixture of apple jelly, honey mustard, apple juice, and brown sugar. The roast teams nicely with Pecan-Glazed Brussels Sprouts. The sprouts take on a sweet taste when glazed with a mixture of brown sugar and toasted pecans.

Pecan-Glazed Brussels Sprouts

Here are two hints to make brussels sprouts more appealing. First, start with tiny, fresh brussels sprouts; you will find them much more tender and less bitter than the larger ones. Second, use your knife to make a shallow "X" in the base of each sprout; this will help the sprouts cook more evenly.

> 1½ pounds fresh brussels sprouts
> ½ cup water
> ¼ cup unsalted butter or margarine
> ⅓ cup firmly packed brown sugar
> 3 tablespoons soy sauce
> ¼ teaspoon salt
> ½ cup finely chopped pecans, toasted

Wash brussels sprouts thoroughly, and remove discolored leaves. Cut off stem ends and slash bottom of each sprout with a shallow "X." Bring ½ cup water to a boil in a large saucepan; add brussels sprouts. Cover, reduce heat, and simmer 8 to 10 minutes, or until

sprouts are crisp-tender; drain and set aside.

Melt butter in a medium skillet; stir in brown sugar, soy sauce, and salt. Bring butter mixture to a boil, stirring constantly. Add pecans; reduce heat, and simmer, uncovered, 5 minutes, stirring occasionally. Add brussels sprouts; cook over medium heat 5 minutes; stir well before serving.

Yield: 6 servings.

Mary Emma's Ice Box Rolls

These rolls are wonderful served hot from the oven for special occasions.

1 cup water
⅓ cup unsalted butter or margarine
½ cup solid vegetable shortening
¾ cup sugar
1½ teaspoons salt
2 packages active dry yeast
1 cup warm water (105° to 115° F.)
2 eggs, beaten
6 cups all-purpose flour

Combine 1 cup water with the butter, shortening, sugar, and salt in a saucepan; heat over low heat until butter and shortening melt. Let cool until temperature registers 105° to 115° F. on a candy thermometer.

Dissolve yeast in 1 cup warm water in

Mary Emma's Ice Box Rolls are easy to shape. Just cut, crease, and fold.

a large mixing bowl; let stand 5 minutes. Stir in cooled melted shortening mixture and eggs. Gradually add 2 cups flour, beating with an electric mixer on medium speed until smooth. Stir in enough remaining flour to form a thick dough. Turn dough out onto a floured surface, and knead 5 to 8 minutes, or until smooth and elastic. Place in a well-greased bowl, turning to grease top; cover and refrigerate 1½ to 2 hours.

Punch dough down; turn dough out onto a lightly floured surface. Roll to ¼-inch thickness. Cut rounds with a 2½-inch cutter. With the dull edge of knife, make a crease just off center on each round. Fold over so that top overlaps slightly; gently press edges together.

Place on lightly greased baking sheets. Cover and let rise in a warm place (85° F.), free from drafts, for 1 hour, or until doubled in bulk.

Preheat oven to 400° F.

Bake for 12 to 15 minutes, or until golden.

Yield: 3 dozen.

Pantry Chess Pie

It is possible that pecan pie was developed from a chess pie recipe. In any case, it's a mystery as to how chess pie got its name. Perhaps it was called a "chest" pie at first, since early cooks stored their pies in a piece of furniture called a pie chest or pie safe.

> 1½ cups sugar
> 1 tablespoon cornmeal
> ¼ teaspoon salt
> 4 eggs, beaten
> 1½ teaspoons vanilla extract
> ¼ cup milk
> ¼ cup unsalted butter or margarine, melted
> 1 Single-Crust Pie Pastry (page 42), unbaked

Preheat oven to 350° F.

Combine sugar, cornmeal, and salt in a small bowl; mix well. Combine eggs and vanilla in a medium bowl; beat well. Add sugar mixture, milk, and butter to egg mixture; beat until smooth.

Line a 9-inch pie plate with pastry; trim and flute edges. Pour in filling. Bake for 30 minutes, or until set.

Yield: 6 to 8 servings.

Gingerbread Cake with Lemon Sauce

This gingerbread is often referred to as a "hot water" cake, since hot water is added for moisture. You can dress up this simple dessert by spooning lemon sauce over each serving.

> ½ cup unsalted butter or margarine
> ¼ cup sugar
> ¼ cup firmly packed brown sugar
> 1 egg, beaten
> ⅔ cup light molasses

Chess pie was popular during the time when dessert depended on the creativity of a housewife working with ordinary farm staples—sugar, eggs, butter, and milk. Like most chess pies, Pantry Chess Pie puffs slightly as it bakes but sinks when removed from the oven.

2 ¼ cups all-purpose flour
1 ½ teaspoons baking soda
½ teaspoon salt
2 teaspoons ground ginger
½ teaspoon ground nutmeg
½ teaspoon ground cinnamon
¼ teaspoon ground cloves
1 cup hot water

Lemon Sauce:

½ cup sugar
1 tablespoon cornstarch
1 cup boiling water
2 tablespoons unsalted butter or
   margarine
2 tablespoons lemon juice
1 teaspoon grated lemon rind

Preheat oven to 350° F.

Cream butter with an electric mixer on low speed. Gradually add sugar and brown sugar, beating on medium speed until light and fluffy. Add egg and molasses, mixing well. Combine flour, soda, salt, and spices; add to creamed mixture alternately with hot water, beginning and ending with flour mixture. Mix well.

Pour batter into a lightly greased and floured 9-inch-square baking pan. Bake for 35 minutes, or until a wooden pick inserted in center comes out clean. Let cool completely in pan on a wire rack. Cut into squares or wedges to serve.

To make sauce, combine sugar and cornstarch in a small saucepan. Gradu-

ally stir in boiling water. Cook over low heat, stirring constantly, until smooth and thickened. Remove from heat; add butter, lemon juice, and lemon rind, stirring until butter melts. Serve over gingerbread squares.

Yield: 9 servings.

Gingerbread Cake with Lemon Sauce is a dark, moist cake flavored with molasses and ginger and other spices. The cake is baked in a square pan; to serve, cut into squares or wedges and top with tangy lemon sauce.

*T*his brunch for two calls for a cozy fireplace and a table filled with endearing treasures. Since the menu is relaxed but special, you will want to dispense with everyday breakfast dishes and put your wedding china and best silver and crystal to work.

The menu gets off to a sweet start with cups of ambrosia. The fruit is followed with hearty bacon roll-ups, grits-and-sausage casserole, and croissants spread with preserves or marmalade (busy cooks can substitute croissants from the bakery). For an impressive finish, serve baked custards, heart-shaped cookies, champagne, and coffee.

VALENTINE BRUNCH

Mama's Ambrosia

Bacon Roll-Ups

Grits-and-Sausage Casserole

New Orleans—Style Croissants

Individual Baked Custards

Valentine Heart Cookies

Pink Champagne ◆ Café au Lait

Mama's Ambrosia

This is a simple dessert that my mother has always made and served for dessert after holiday dinners. It is also a delicious side dish for breakfast or brunch. I've seen many variations, but the recipe below is ambrosia in its truest form.

8 navel oranges
1 (8-ounce) can pineapple tidbits, drained
2 tablespoons confectioners' sugar
¾ cup flaked coconut
⅓ cup halved maraschino cherries

Peel oranges. Section oranges over a small bowl to catch juice; cut orange sections in half. Set juice aside. Combine oranges and pineapple in a large bowl. Sprinkle with sugar, coconut, and cherries; toss gently until combined. Pour ¼ cup reserved orange juice over mixture. Cover and refrigerate until serving time.

Yield: 6 to 8 servings.

Mama's Ambrosia is a great recipe for winter meals, since oranges are so plentiful during this season.

Bacon Roll-Ups

There was a time when bacon was salt-cured and hickory-smoked on the farm, but today it is generally processed fresh at the slaughterhouse and purchased at the grocery store. The characteristic taste of bacon makes this one of the best cocktail snacks I have ever sampled.

2 (3-ounce) packages cream cheese,
    softened
2 tablespoons grated onion
1 tablespoon milk
1 teaspoon mayonnaise
25 slices whole-wheat sandwich bread,
    cut in half, crusts removed
25 slices bacon, cut in half

Preheat oven to 350° F.

Combine cream cheese, onion, milk, and mayonnaise, stirring until smooth. Spread cream cheese mixture evenly on each slice of bread. Starting at the short end, roll each slice up tightly. Wrap each roll-up with half a slice of bacon, securing with a wooden pick.

Place roll-ups on a broiler pan; bake for 30 minutes, turning, if needed, to brown bacon. Drain on paper towels.

Yield: 50 appetizers.

Grits-and-Sausage Casserole

Stone-ground grits, made by grinding mature corn kernels, are still available in some areas of the South. This recipe uses quick-cooking grits, which can be purchased in most grocery stores.

1 cup uncooked quick-cooking grits
1 pound mild bulk pork sausage
8 eggs, beaten
1½ cups milk
¼ teaspoon garlic salt
¼ teaspoon white pepper
3 tablespoons lightly salted butter or
    margarine
2 cups (8 ounces) shredded sharp
    Cheddar cheese

Cook grits according to package directions. Set aside.

Cook sausage over medium heat until browned, stirring to crumble. Drain well and set aside.

Preheat oven to 350° F.

Combine eggs, milk, garlic salt, and white pepper in a large bowl. Stir in cooked grits. Add butter and cheese, stirring until cheese melts. Stir in sausage. Spoon mixture into a lightly greased 3-quart casserole. Bake, uncovered, for 1 hour, or until set.

Yield: 8 servings.

New Orleans–Style Croissants

The French bakeries in New Orleans are responsible for making these buttery rolls so popular in the South. They are delicious served for breakfast with your favorite jam or marmalade.

1 package dry yeast
¼ cup warm water (105° to 115° F.)
¾ cup milk
2 tablespoons sugar
¾ cup plus 1 tablespoon unsalted
  butter
1 teaspoon salt
1 egg, beaten
3½ to 3¾ cups all-purpose flour

Dissolve yeast in warm water; let stand 5 minutes.

Place milk in a small saucepan. Cook over medium heat, until thoroughly heated (about 180° F. on a candy thermometer), but not boiling. Combine milk, sugar, 1 tablespoon of the butter, and salt in a large bowl; mix well. Cool to 105° to 115° F. on a candy thermometer. Add egg and yeast mixture, mixing well. Gradually stir in enough flour to make a soft dough. Place in a well-greased bowl; turn to grease top. Cover; chill 1 hour.

Place dough on a lightly floured surface; roll out into a 12-inch square. Spread ¼ cup of the remaining butter evenly over dough. Fold corners to center; then fold dough in half. Wrap in plastic wrap and refrigerate 30 minutes. Repeat rolling, buttering, and folding procedure twice; cover and refrigerate at least 1 hour.

Divide dough in half; roll each half into a 14-inch circle on a lightly floured surface; cut into 6 wedges. Roll up each wedge, beginning at the wide end. Seal points; place croissants point side down on greased baking sheets; let rise in a warm place (85° F.), free from drafts, for 1 hour, or until doubled in bulk.

Preheat oven to 400° F.

Bake for 12 minutes, or until lightly browned.

Yield: 12 croissants.

New Orleans–Style Croissants are traditionally thought of as breakfast pastries, but they can also be split for a sandwich or served as rolls at dinner meals.

Individual Baked Custards

This is my favorite dessert. I like it because the flavor is sweet but not too sweet, and the texture is as smooth as velvet.

> 2 cups milk
> 3 eggs
> ½ cup sugar
> 1 teaspoon vanilla extract
> ¼ teaspoon salt
> Freshly grated nutmeg
> Melted semisweet chocolate (optional)

Place milk in top of a double boiler; bring water underneath to a boil. Cook until milk is thoroughly heated (about 180° F. on a candy thermometer), but not boiling. Set aside.

Preheat oven to 350° F.

Beat eggs until frothy. Add sugar, vanilla, and salt; beat well. Gradually stir about ½ cup hot milk into egg mixture; add egg mixture to remaining milk, stirring constantly.

Pour egg mixture evenly into six lightly greased (6-ounce) custard cups. Sprinkle each custard lightly with nutmeg. Make a water bath by placing cups in a 13- x 9- x 2-inch baking dish; add hot water to baking dish to a depth of 1 inch up sides of dish. Bake for 45 to 50 minutes, or until a knife inserted in center of a custard comes out clean. Remove cups from water bath; let cool. Refrigerate custards 4 hours.

Individual Baked Custards are superb eaten directly from the custard cups or inverted onto dessert plates. But for a truly impressive presentation, the custard can be inverted onto a pool of melted chocolate and garnished with a chocolate heart. The hearts are made by drizzling melted chocolate onto a wax paper–lined baking sheet. After freezing, the designs can be gently removed and placed on top of the custards.

Custards may be served directly from custard cups or inverted onto individual dessert plates. If a fancier presentation is desired, you may fill a pastry decorating bag, fitted with a small tip, with melted chocolate. Drizzle heart designs on wax paper on a baking sheet; freeze until firm. Pool a small amount of melted chocolate on each dessert plate. Gently invert custards onto chocolate sauce. Let frozen chocolate heart designs come to room temperature; gently lift off designs and place on top of custards.

Yield: 6 servings.

Valentine Heart Cookies

Sour cream gives this cookie dough rich flavor. Cut the cookies into hearts and sprinkle them with sugar; they are certain to win your loved one's favor. For best results, work with only one third of dough at a time. Also, wipe baking sheets clean between each batch of cookies.

1 cup sugar
1 cup solid vegetable shortening
1 egg
1 (8-ounce) container sour cream
1 teaspoon vanilla extract
4¾ cups all-purpose flour
1 teaspoon baking powder
1 teaspoon baking soda
¼ teaspoon salt
Red decorator sugar crystals

In a large bowl, combine sugar, shortening, and egg; beat with an electric mixer on low speed until light and fluffy. Add sour cream and vanilla, mixing well. Combine flour, baking powder, soda, and salt; add to creamed mixture, beating well. Cover dough with plastic wrap. Chill dough at least 1 hour.

Preheat oven to 350° F.

Divide dough into thirds; work with one third of dough at a time, keeping remaining dough covered and refrigerated. Roll dough out onto a lightly floured surface to ⅛-inch thickness; cut into heart shapes using a 2- to 3-inch heart cutter. Place cookies on ungreased baking sheets; sprinkle with red sugar crystals. Bake for 10 to 12 minutes, or until lightly browned. Remove from pan and cool on wire racks.

Yield: 7 to 8 dozen cookies.

Valentine Heart Cookies bake into crisp, crunchy wafers. Red sugar crystals are sprinkled on the cookies before they are baked. The cookies are accompanied by cups of hot café au lait. Traditionally served in Louisiana kitchens, café au lait is made by combining very dark, strong coffee with an equal amount of steaming milk.

Spring

Outdoors at Last

Spring dresses the roads with dogwoods and
azaleas and tiny buds emerge against green leaves.
The weather sends days that should never end, and windows
and doors open to inhale a fresh breath. We clean
and polish and bring out our finest as we
sniff the amazingly sweet air.

Left: Like a group of shy young girls, these short-cupped daffodils cling together, peering out at the spring sun. ♦ *Center: For a unified garden, it is best to plant tulips in groups of a single color. For more than one color, gently run the groups together, or plant separate color groups in different areas. It is also a good idea*

Spring begins to tease us weeks before her arrival. For a few days in February, breezes whisper in the trees, and the sky turns gentle blue. We think about storing our sweaters and dream of trips to the beach. We wonder when the bulbs hibernating in the garden will shoot forth their colors.

But after this respite, Old Man Winter reminds us that he intends to stay a bit longer. It

to plant the tulips amid low-growing, early spring flowers—Johnny-jump-ups, pansies, or forget-me-nots—
that will continue to bloom when the tulip foliage begins to die down. ⬧ Right: No flowers proclaim spring
with more eloquence than yellow daffodils and blue hyacinths.

drizzles on and off, and the cold weather sputters along until it is finally overtaken by spring in the waning days of March.

This season of renewal sometimes catches us by pleasant surprise. Wrapped up in our everyday activities, we suddenly realize that the forsythia has burst forth in tiny yellow petals, its branches bending in long, willowy waves. Sunny daffodils pop up by the dozens, insistent reminders that

balmy days have returned. Pale green leaves unfurl to clothe branches that shivered all winter. Stepping outside becomes pure joy.

The days begin to stretch, allowing precious hours to stroll or cycle through the neighborhood. The fussy chirps of nesting birds and the laughter of barefoot children down the street lead us to thoughts of barbecues, picnics, afternoon softball games, and fishing.

On the Southern farm, calves, baby chicks, and piglets are born. Important crops—corn, green beans, watermelon, and peanuts—are planted. And later, tender English peas, slender stalks of asparagus, and sweet strawberries are picked and enjoyed.

Spring is a busy season, but we Southerners still find time for special get-togethers—Easter-egg hunts, wedding teas, baby showers, and christenings. These are the occasions when Southern hospitality reigns supreme.

One of the first signs of a Southern spring is when the lacy dogwood trees begin to bloom. The small flowering trees are prevalent all over the South; they are often part of a planned landscape, but they can also be spotted growing wild along roadsides, in meadows, and beside riverbanks. Each spring the green, oval dogwood leaves provide a background for the familiar white or pink blooms. The flowers are typically composed of four large white bracts, or petals, that are magenta-tinged and slightly notched at the tips. Dogwood trails in many cities and towns provide popular entertainment for Sunday afternoon outings.

Dressy linens are starched and pressed. Silver is polished, and crystal is washed until it sparkles.

On special occasions you might find a roasted hen, a marinated beef tenderloin, or a baked ham on the menu. We look forward to May, when sweet Vidalia onions are sliced and savored, and tiny new potatoes are scrubbed and coated in cream sauce.

Spring desserts, although more casual, are every bit as delicious and rich as winter desserts. The popularity of pineapple upside-down cake, strawberry shortcake, and lemon meringue pie never seems to fade.

No other season draws us outside like spring. After a filling dinner and dessert, we find ourselves seeking the comfort of a porch swing. As dusk settles, voices murmur, and ice clinks in tall glasses of tea. Talk is of the familiar—compliments to the cook, the peach crop, yesterday's rain and tomorrow's blue sky.

Above: Each spring, two large flowering pear trees bloom in front of the Martin-Smith-Davis house in Mooresville, Alabama. Standing beside a white picket fence, the robust trees form a bright display of white blossoms for any guests that might drop by for a visit. ♦ Above right: Walk down the side streets of almost any small Southern town in the early morning or late evening and you will surely hear the soft squeak of chains as the time-honored porch swing moves gently back and forth. The wooden porch swing, sort of an outdoor sofa, has always been a natural landing spot whenever there was a pan of peas to shell, a book to read, a problem to mull over, news to share with a neighbor, or a sweetheart to court. ♦ Right: Window boxes possess an eye-catching charm all their own. The key to a successful window box is choosing a plant or combination of plants that will do well in the amount of sun or shade that the box receives. Jeanne Rogers, of Birmingham, has created a shaded windowscape by mixing caladiums, jasmine, ivy, and marigolds.

Expecting Company

Early on, Southern mothers instill in their daughters a love of entertaining. Girls first learn this art by helping to polish silver or prepare dainty sandwiches before a party. Their efforts are often rewarded with a sampling of peppery cheese wafers or tea cookies. But one of their greatest pleasures comes in helping to set an elegant table with fresh flowers, creamy linens and lace, gleaming silver, and sparkling crystal and china.

During the Victorian era, fine linens and lace became the hall-

Opposite: A collection of pale pink sherbet glasses sparkle in the afternoon sun. The crystal glasses are arranged on a cupid mirrored tray. ♦ Inset: The Limoges area of France, about 230 miles southwest of Paris, has long been regarded as the chief porcelain center of Europe. This Limoges vegetable bowl with raised paste gilding might have appeared on most any well-to-do Southern family's table during the late 1800s. ♦ Above: The picket fence as we know it today is probably a descendant of the paling fences used for protection in seventeenth-century settlements. As time passed, the fences assumed new roles—to enclose a garden or yard or simply as an ornamental feature. Barbara DeBank's summer home in Beaufort, North Carolina, was built in 1912 but is surrounded today by a delicately undulating white-painted picket fence.

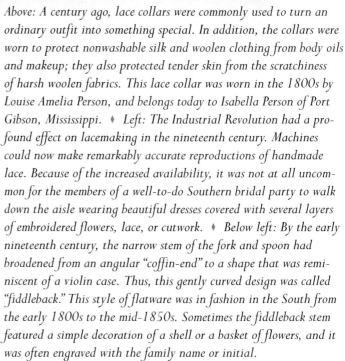

Above: A century ago, lace collars were commonly used to turn an ordinary outfit into something special. In addition, the collars were worn to protect nonwashable silk and woolen clothing from body oils and makeup; they also protected tender skin from the scratchiness of harsh woolen fabrics. This lace collar was worn in the 1800s by Louise Amelia Person, and belongs today to Isabella Person of Port Gibson, Mississippi. ♦ Left: The Industrial Revolution had a profound effect on lacemaking in the nineteenth century. Machines could now make remarkably accurate reproductions of handmade lace. Because of the increased availability, it was not at all uncommon for the members of a well-to-do Southern bridal party to walk down the aisle wearing beautiful dresses covered with several layers of embroidered flowers, lace, or cutwork. ♦ Below left: By the early nineteenth century, the narrow stem of the fork and spoon had broadened from an angular "coffin-end" to a shape that was reminiscent of a violin case. Thus, this gently curved design was called "fiddleback." This style of flatware was in fashion in the South from the early 1800s to the mid-1850s. Sometimes the fiddleback stem featured a simple decoration of a shell or a basket of flowers, and it was often engraved with the family name or initial.

mark of every well-appointed Southern home. Linen napkins were often numbered or monogrammed to aid in identification during cleaning. Homemakers would assign a napkin ring and napkin to each member of the family, a practice that still continues in some households, especially when a large group sits down to three meals on Sunday.

Lace did not become readily accessible until the nineteenth century and the advent of machine-made lace. Thus the former luxury item became a middle-class commodity, and Southerners

Above: The Burn is one of the oldest Greek Revival residences in Natchez, Mississippi. When touring the mansion's dining room, most visitors are intrigued by the flower-patterned Haviland china that is displayed on the dining table. This 110-piece china service is believed to have been made before 1850, and includes large platters for fish and meat, covered vegetable bowls, and pôts de crème cups. ♦ Above right: A vogue for objects made of silver and glass occurred during the late nineteenth and early twentieth centuries. The materials were combined by a process called silver-depositing or silver-mounting. Typically, the delicate fruit, flower, and abstract designs were also enhanced with engraving or etching. Popular articles made in silver deposit and silver mount included decanters, flasks, pitchers, cigarette boxes, picture frames, and vases. ♦ Below right: The dining table of Monmouth in Natchez, Mississippi, remains impressively set with hand-painted Sèvres china, silver-plated English goblets, and unique pewter napkin rings. Each of the napkin rings sports a different animal shape, and each of the china plates features a different love scene. While the china dates to the late 1700s, the silver and pewter pieces would have appeared in the mid-1800s.

Above left: Cruet stands fitted with cruets and casters are highly prized in the South today, mostly because it is unusual to find a set that still contains all the original pieces. The sets typically held two or more cut-glass cruet bottles with silver tops for oil and vinegar and two or more silver casters for various spices, usually salt and pepper. ♦ *Above right: Between 1880 and 1915 cut glass began to be produced in America on a large scale. Because of this, cut glass enjoyed a popularity that flourished especially in the South, where the heavy vases, pitchers, and bowls were treasured. Glass collectors refer to this time frame as the "brilliant" period, because technological improvements allowed for the production of glass that was purer, more brilliant, and cut more precisely. These three highly prized vases feature cut geometric patterns that were commonly used during this period.*

began to place lace doilies on tables, lace scarves on dressers, and frilly pillowcases on the bed.

Silver has always been treasured in the South. The earliest Southerners ordered their silver from England, but eventually silversmiths in our region began to make flatware from coin silver. A wide variety of utensils might have appeared in the well-to-do Southerner's flatware inventory, including oyster forks, butter knifes, soup and dessert spoons, or even a fish slicer.

After about 1860, pieces of solid silver were identified as sterling. Flatware in matching sets with serving pieces, tea sets, ornate candelabra, pitchers, and vases enjoyed popularity and were produced in quantity.

It is not surprising that crystal has long graced Southern dining tables. In the early 1800s, cut glass featured simple patterns, such as flutes; cutting was not emphasized as much as engraving and etching were. But near the end of the nineteenth century, cut glass became more detailed, featuring geometric designs that were given names. Later, nature inspired craftsmen to use plants, birds, and insects in their designs.

The appreciation of fine china has been handed down for generations, to which collections in Southern historic homes and museums attest. Southern planters and their descendants set the standard for gracious living. In addition to Oriental chinaware, they ordered pieces from Europe—those of Old Paris, Limoges, Sèvres, Haviland, Meissen, Worcester, Wedgwood, and others.

Left: Much of the tableware that has been handed down in Southern families dates from the mid-nineteenth to early twentieth centuries. About this time, production of porcelain and fine earthenware reached its peak, and well-to-do Southern brides began to order tableware from overseas. Settings for twelve to twenty were not uncommon, and would often include special settings for dessert in addition to dinner. Formal dining rooms were also becoming more fashionable, and with them came the corner cabinet, a place to store and display the valuable tableware and porcelain. ♦ Top right: Cut-glass berry bowls were often used in the South for serving fruit, salad, or vegetables. Interestingly, most of the geometric patterns that were featured on cut-glass items of this period were given names. The cut design on this bowl bears a resemblance to a pattern known as Zenda, which is a combination of deep fans and alternating triangles of cross-hatching and strawberry-diamond cuts. This pattern was not as expensive to cut as some of the more intricate star patterns, and it was featured in a variety of decanters, tumblers, and goblets. ♦ Lower right: During the late nineteenth century, large silver manufacturers created an extensive array of silver objects that relatives and friends traditionally lavished on newborn children. While the baby might receive a silver rattle or teething ring, cups and mugs and eating utensils were the most popular gifts. Children's eating sets were both practical and ornamental, and cups such as this one were often displayed as part of the family silver.

Bursting Forth

Few sights are more glorious than the South in full bloom. Each spring, "Sunday drivers," prone to take their time on weekend outings, drive even more slowly to admire the scenery. They pass plenty of azaleas—blooming white, scarlet, crimson, and purple—in banks across Southern lawns. Dogwood "trails" lead drivers past lacy stands of dogwood trees, with white blossoms

Opposite: Although tulips are classified as perennials, some Southern gardeners have a difficult time keeping the same bulbs blooming year after year because the weather is just too warm. Many gardeners in the Deep South grow tulips as annuals—when the blooms are gone, the plants are dug up and discarded and new ones replanted each fall. In spite of this, tulips are a special part of a Southern spring, for their bold, brilliant colors help start the season on a cheerful note. ♦ Inset: Butterfly weed, a relative of milkweed, has bright orange, red, or yellow flowers and grows well in dry or sandy soils. The rough, hairy stems and leaves do not contain milky juice as the other members of the milkweed family do. ♦ Above: There are many varieties of flowering cherry trees in the South; most are small trees, but they do include different forms and varying leaf and flower characteristics. Although the trees are very handsome, they are usually considered inferior to dogwoods or crabapples because they are prone to borer damage and are often quite short-lived.

perched ever so slightly on branches, like a fresh, unexpected snow.

Other flowering trees, such as magnolia, cherry, crabapple, and pear, also ornament Southern lawns. Some, like the great magnolia, have blossoms that emit a wonderful sweet fragrance.

There are plenty of flowering shrubs to see—deutzia, spiraea, and rhododendron, a native shrub found in mountainous areas near streams. Wildflowers are spotted in moist, shady areas or along the sides of roads and in sunny meadows.

The heavy, woody vines of wisteria are a sight to behold; the violet, white, or pink blossoms grow luxuriantly, some-

Above left: Streaks of blue-to-purple wildflowers spreading loosely across dry wooded or sloping areas will often turn out to be phlox. The pert, small flowers can be identified by their tiny reddish-purple centers. ♦ *Above: Even though wisteria is beautiful, it does grow rampantly; its tendrils quickly engulf any available support and can eventually cause damage. It is wise to train wisteria away from trees, gutters, and wooden trellises; the best supports are brick walls and strong iron fences.* ♦ *Left: Spring in the South is synonymous with colorful masses of azaleas. The flowers have a remarkable color range: white, yellow, orange, scarlet, crimson, and purple, with many intermediate hues of varying intensities.*

times hanging in clusters as long as one foot. And the vivid hues of pert tulips, daffodils, crocuses, and hyacinths are a sure sign of the end of winter.

One of the most exciting sights to witness is that of a blossoming peach orchard. From a distance, the trees stand row on row, as neatly as soldiers. Each trunk seems to split into several branches that shoot out; some have grown gnarly. But a closer look reveals pale blossoms that soften the rigid pattern of the orchard and brush the sky.

Weeks later, peaches hang on the trees, their golden-reddish tones highlighted by spots of yellow and broken by the characteristic cleft. Just the barest fuzz shadows their rich color.

Of course, the real treat comes in late spring and early summer, when the peaches are picked. Southerners look forward to their yearly allotment of peach cobblers and pies, but their hands-down favorite is certainly homemade peach ice cream.

Left: Peaches have always been a major commercial crop in the South, particularly in South Carolina, Georgia, and Alabama. The trees are generally in full bloom by early spring and begin to bear ripe fruit by the first of May. ✦ *Above: The first peaches in the South came from Persia and China. But since Colonial days, Southerners have grown a small seedling clingstone peach called the Indian peach, which reportedly came from Spain. Today some thirty or more varieties of peach trees are planted here. Since peaches will not ripen correctly after they have been picked, it is important to harvest the fruit when it is firm but ripe.*

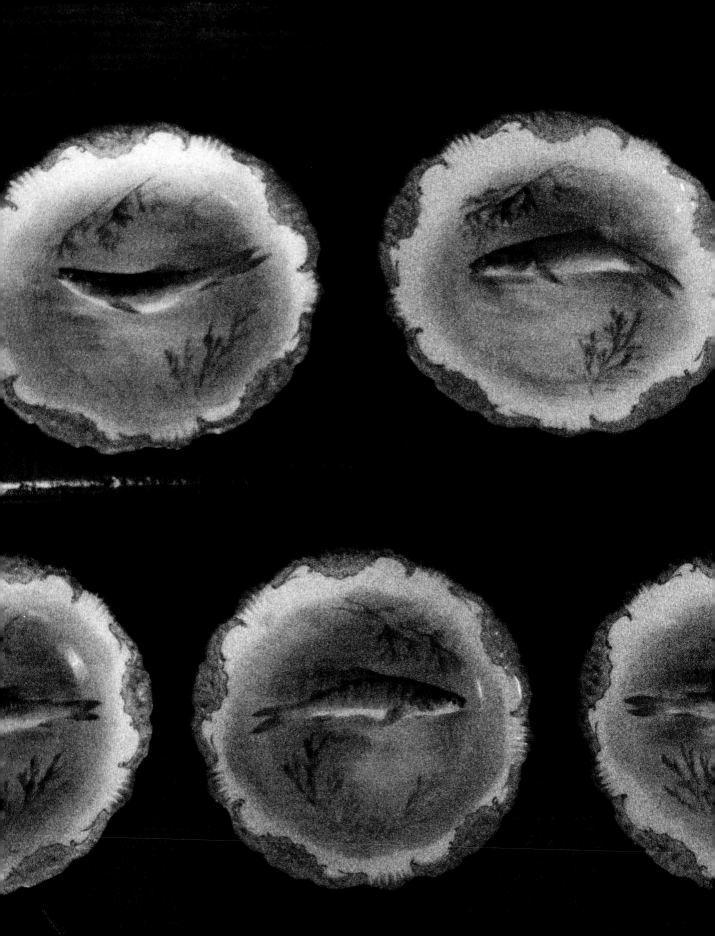

Spring Recipes
Spring's Rewards

MEAT AND FISH

With the arrival of spring's edible gifts we begin to plan menus around the freshest foods of the season. We bid farewell to hearty soups and stews and get ready for fresh, tasty meals making use of spring's bounty.

A large luncheon buffet on a sunny day is a great time to serve a glazed, baked ham or a marinated tenderloin. Casual outdoor gatherings will often revolve around barbecuing pork or grilling chicken. And pan-fried rainbow trout is perfect for an intimate dinner for two.

Pan-Glazed Rainbow Trout

The creeks, streams, and rivers of the Smoky Mountains and Blue Ridge Mountains provide fly fishermen with solitude and an unending bounty of fish. But the best part of a fisherman's day is when he savors his catch.

2 whole, cleaned rainbow trout (about 1½ pounds)
¼ cup all-purpose flour
½ teaspoon salt
½ teaspoon black pepper
⅛ teaspoon paprika
⅛ teaspoon garlic powder
4 tablespoons unsalted butter, melted
¼ cup slivered almonds
1 teaspoon brown sugar

Rinse fish under cold water; pat dry.

Combine flour, salt, pepper, paprika, and garlic powder in a large bowl. Dredge fish in flour mixture; shake off excess. Fry fish in 2 tablespoons of the butter in a large cast-iron skillet 5 minutes on each side, or until golden. Transfer to a serving dish.

Add remaining 2 tablespoons butter to skillet. Add almonds and brown sugar; sauté until golden. Spoon almonds and butter-sugar glaze over fish. Serve immediately.

Yield: 2 servings.

Honey-Glazed Ham

This ham is so moist and delicious that each slice practically melts in your mouth. The sweet outer coating teams nicely with the saltiness of the ham.

1 (6- to 8-pound) smoked, fully cooked bone-in ham half

Glaze:
⅔ cup firmly packed brown sugar
⅓ cup sugar
1½ teaspoons ground nutmeg
1 teaspoon ground cloves
½ teaspoon ground cinnamon
½ cup honey

Preheat oven to 325° F.

Remove hard outer skin from ham, leaving a thin layer of fat; place ham, fat side up, on a rack in a shallow roasting pan. With a sharp knife, score fat in a diamond design; insert meat thermometer into ham, making sure it does not touch fat or bone. Bake ham for 1 hour and 15 minutes. Remove ham; leave oven on.

Combine the sugars and spices, stirring well. Brush ham generously with honey. Pat brown-sugar mixture over honey, coating ham thoroughly. Return ham to oven, and bake at 325° F. for 30 to 40 minutes, or until meat thermometer registers 140° F.

Yield: 12 to 14 servings.

Marinated Beef Tenderloin

When Southern cooks need to serve an impressive main course, they often turn to beef tenderloin. This is the same dish I served for our son's christening luncheon.

Marinade:

 1 ¼ cups port wine
 ½ cup vegetable oil
 ¼ cup lemon juice
 ¼ cup Worcestershire sauce
 ¼ cup water
 2 teaspoons black pepper
 1 teaspoon dried thyme leaves
 1 teaspoon hot sauce
 4 cloves garlic, crushed
 1 bay leaf

 1 (5- to 6-pound) beef tenderloin, trimmed

Combine all the ingredients for the marinade; mix well. Place tenderloin in a large shallow dish and pour marinade over. Cover tightly and refrigerate overnight.

Preheat oven to 425° F.

Uncover tenderloin; drain off and reserve marinade. Heat marinade in a small saucepan until it comes to a full boil; discard bay leaf. Set marinade aside.

Place tenderloin on a rack in a pan; insert meat thermometer, making sure it does not touch fat. Bake for 45 to 60 minutes, or until thermometer registers 140° F. (rare), basting occasionally with marinade. Remove to serving platter; serve remaining marinade on the side.

Yield: 10 to 12 servings.

Marinated Beef Tenderloin looks pretty garnished with enoki and shiitake mushrooms, fresh dill, rosemary, basil, and thyme. But it would also look nice served over a bed of rice or surrounded with cooked fresh vegetables.

Some Southern cooks spell it "barbecue." Others prefer "Bar-B-Q." But it seems that almost all cooks like their pork ribs roasted to perfection and brushed with a thick, tangy, tomato-and-vinegar-based sauce.

Best Barbecued Ribs

Good barbecued ribs are revered in the South. In fact, I have even heard of Southerners paying off debts with barbecued ribs rather than money. All barbecue experts have tips to share, but two of the best are to cook ribs over a slow fire, and to add the sauce during the last 30 minutes of cooking.

4 pounds pork back ribs or spare ribs

Spice Rub:

    1 tablespoon paprika
    1 teaspoon salt
    1 teaspoon black pepper
    1 teaspoon garlic powder
    1 teaspoon cayenne pepper

Barbecue Sauce:

    ¼ cup catsup
    ¼ cup red wine vinegar
    ¼ cup tomato sauce
    2 tablespoons honey mustard
    1 tablespoon Worcestershire sauce
    1 tablespoon unsalted butter or
      margarine
    1 teaspoon hot sauce
    1 teaspoon lemon juice
    1 teaspoon brown sugar
    ½ teaspoon salt
    ¼ teaspoon garlic powder
    ⅛ teaspoon chili powder
    ⅛ teaspoon cayenne pepper
    ⅛ teaspoon black pepper

Basting Liquid:

    ½ cup red wine vinegar
    ½ cup water
    1 tablespoon brown sugar

Place ribs in a large, shallow roasting pan. Combine spice-rub ingredients in a small bowl; stir well. Rub spice mixture over ribs. Cover pan with aluminum foil and refrigerate ribs 4 hours or overnight.

Meanwhile, in a small saucepan, combine barbecue-sauce ingredients and bring to a boil. Cook, stirring often, 15 to 20 minutes. Set sauce mixture aside.

Preheat oven to 300° F.

Bake ribs, covered, for 1 hour. Drain ribs.

Heat a charcoal or gas grill. Combine red wine vinegar, ½ cup water, and brown sugar, stirring well. Place ribs over 300° to 350° F. coals (slow coals) and cook for 15 minutes, basting with vinegar mixture and turning ribs occasionally.

Brush ribs with barbecue sauce; cook 10 to 15 minutes, turning ribs and brushing with sauce occasionally.

Yield: 3 to 4 servings.

With the appearance of fresh onions, peas, and new potatoes, the garden begins a slow crescendo which will climax in the summer with tomatoes, green beans, corn, and squash. It's a wonderful time— one that every gardener looks forward to.

VEGETABLES AND SALADS

As spring days begin to lengthen, the sun's rays gently coax fresh vegetables from carefully tended gardens. Spring is a major planting and growing season, but some wonderful treasures can be harvested, too—tiny new potatoes, pencil-thin stalks of asparagus, brilliant-green English peas, and mild, sweet onions.

The vegetables of spring are so delicate and flavorful that they are best prepared very simply. Many can be just cleaned and sliced and tossed directly into salads. Others—like potatoes and onions—are often sautéed or topped with a cream sauce. Still others—asparagus and peas—might be quickly steamed.

Garden Club Perfection Salad

Gelatin salads have always been popular with Southern cooks. I sometimes suspect they secretly compete with one another to come up with new combinations of ingredients for their shimmering masterpieces. The salad below is a classic; it is often the star of the table at neighborhood garden club meetings.

2 envelopes unflavored gelatin
½ cup cold water
2 cups boiling water
¼ cup sugar
¼ cup lemon juice
¼ cup cider vinegar
¼ teaspoon salt
1 cup grated carrots
1 (15¼-ounce) can crushed
　pineapple, drained
¾ cup finely shredded cabbage
⅓ cup chopped green bell pepper
1 (2-ounce) jar diced pimiento,
　drained

Combine gelatin and ½ cup cold water in a medium bowl; add 2 cups boiling water, stirring until gelatin dis-

solves. Add sugar, lemon juice, vinegar, and salt; stir well. Chill until the consistency of unbeaten egg white.

Gently fold carrot, pineapple, cabbage, green pepper, and pimiento into gelatin mixture. Pour gelatin mixture into a lightly oiled 5-cup mold. Cover and chill until firm. Unmold to serve.

Yield: 6 servings.

Garden Club Perfection Salad is filled with colorful grated carrots, crushed pineapple, shredded cabbage, and chopped green pepper.

Vidalia Gourmet

Vidalia onions are harvested once a year and are usually available in the market sometime around the first of May. The flat-topped yellow onion gets its sweet flavor from the low sulfur content of the soil of Vidalia, Georgia, and surrounding counties.

> 5 medium Vidalia onions, sliced
> ⅓ cup unsalted butter or margarine, melted
> 1 teaspoon sugar
> ½ teaspoon salt
> ½ teaspoon black pepper
> ½ cup dry sherry
> 2 dashes hot sauce
> 2 tablespoons grated Parmesan cheese

Sherry, hot sauce, and Parmesan cheese add flavor to Vidalia Gourmet. True Vidalia onions will quite often, though not always, have a sticker identifying them as such.

Sauté onion slices in butter in a Dutch oven over medium heat for 5 to 8 minutes, or until crisp-tender. Sprinkle with sugar, salt, and pepper; stir gently to separate into rings. Add sherry and hot sauce; simmer 2 to 3 minutes. Sprinkle with cheese and serve immediately.

Yield: 6 to 8 servings.

New Potatoes in Cream Sauce

During the Depression, plain boiled potatoes were served up almost every day. As times improved, the ordinary potato gained new status—it was mashed or whipped with butter and cream into great mounds or partially peeled and tossed in a rich cream sauce, as here.

> 12 new potatoes
> 3 tablespoons unsalted butter or margarine
> 3 tablespoons all-purpose flour
> ½ teaspoon salt
> ¼ teaspoon white pepper
> 1 cup milk
> ½ cup half-and-half

Garnish:
> 1 tablespoon chopped fresh chives

When making New Potatoes in Cream Sauce, remember to use only small, waxy potatoes. It is typical, though not necessary, to remove the peeling of the potatoes, either entirely or just around the middle.

Wash potatoes; pare a 1-inch strip around center of each potato. Place potatoes in a large saucepan; cover with water and bring to a boil over medium heat. Cover, reduce heat, and simmer 15 to 20 minutes, or until potatoes are tender; drain well.

Melt butter in a heavy saucepan over low heat; add flour, salt, and pepper, stirring until smooth. Cook 1 minute, stirring constantly. Gradually stir in milk and half-and-half; cook over medium heat, stirring constantly, until thickened and bubbly. Pour over potatoes; sprinkle with chives.

Yield: 4 servings.

Celery and sliced water chestnuts contribute crisp texture to an otherwise creamy English Pea Salad. The salad looks pretty served in a bowl lined with lettuce or cabbage leaves and garnished with an onion fan.

English Pea Salad

A bowl of English peas, seasoned with butter and black pepper, always appeared on our Sunday dinner table. Only later did I discover that these tiny green peas are also quite tasty served chilled in a sour cream and mayonnaise dressing.

> 2 (17-ounce) cans English peas, drained, or 3 (10-ounce) packages frozen tiny green peas, thawed
> 2 cups finely chopped celery
> 1 (8-ounce) can sliced water chestnuts, drained
> 1 (4-ounce) jar diced pimiento, drained
> ½ cup chopped green onions
> ½ cup sour cream
> ½ cup mayonnaise
> ¼ teaspoon salt
> ¼ teaspoon white pepper

Combine peas, celery, water chestnuts, pimiento, and green onions in a large bowl. Combine sour cream and mayonnaise, stirring well. Add sour-cream mixture, salt, and pepper to vegetables; toss gently to coat. Cover and chill thoroughly.

Yield: 6 to 8 servings.

The warmer temperatures and rains of spring lead to a steady parade of beautiful blooms which gradually yield to the arrival of sweet fruits and vegetables.

DESSERTS

Spring desserts are as refreshing and beautiful as the season. The hearty flavors of fall and winter are replaced with the delicate taste of fresh, sweet fruits stirred into a variety of cakes, cheesecakes, shortcakes, puddings, meringues, and pies.

When I think of spring desserts, two traditional Southern desserts come to mind. Upside-down cake, similar to a French tarte Tatin, is baked in a cast-iron skillet and inverted onto a serving plate. Strawberry shortcake, made with biscuit-like pastry, is split and layered with whipped cream and berries.

Pineapple Upside-Down Cake

Upside-down cakes, made in black cast-iron skillets, have always been popular in the South. I've seen many variations, including apple, cherry, and ambrosia upside-down cakes, but pineapple is by far the most traditional. Before serving, the baked cake is inverted onto a plate so the glazed fruit becomes the top of the cake.

½ cup unsalted butter or margarine
1 cup firmly packed brown sugar
1 (20-ounce) can pineapple slices, undrained
7 maraschino cherries
12 pecan halves

My mother always liked to make Pineapple Upside-Down Cake when I was growing up, partly because it was convenient—it could be cooked and served from a cast-iron skillet. But the main reason was that it tasted so good, and my father requested it often.

3 egg yolks
1 cup sugar
1 cup all-purpose flour
1 teaspoon baking powder
½ teaspoon salt
1 teaspoon vanilla extract
2 egg whites

Melt butter in a 10-inch cast-iron skillet over low heat. Sprinkle brown sugar in skillet. Remove from heat.

Drain pineapple, reserving ¼ cup juice. Set juice aside. Arrange 7 pineapple slices over sugar mixture. Cut remaining pineapple slices in half; line sides of pan, keeping cut sides up. Place a cherry in the center of each whole pineapple slice; arrange pecan halves between slices in a spoke fashion.

Preheat oven to 350° F.

Beat 3 egg yolks with an electric mixer on medium speed until thick and lemon-colored; gradually add 1 cup sugar, beating well. Combine flour, baking powder, and salt; stir well. Add to egg mixture alternately with reserved pineapple juice, mixing well. Stir in vanilla.

Beat egg whites with an electric mixer on high speed until stiff peaks form; fold beaten egg whites into batter. Spoon batter evenly over pineapple in skillet. Bake for 45 to 50 minutes, or until cake is set. Immediately invert cake onto a serving plate.

Yield: 6 servings.

Slice o' Lemon Pie

The Shakers of Pleasant Hill, Kentucky, were known to prepare lemon pies similar to this one. The recipe is still popular today; I found this one in my mother-in-law's recipe box.

Double-Crust Pie Pastry (page 39)
1⅓ cups plus 1 tablespoon sugar
2 tablespoons all-purpose flour
¼ cup unsalted butter, softened
3 eggs
½ cup water
1 medium lemon, peeled and sliced
paper-thin
1 egg white

Line a 9-inch pie plate with half of pastry and set aside.

Combine 1⅓ cups of the sugar and the flour, stirring well. Cream butter with an electric mixer on low speed; gradually add sugar mixture, beating until light and fluffy. Add eggs, one at a time, and ½ cup water, beating well. Stir in lemon slices; spoon into prepared pastry.

Preheat oven to 400° F.

Roll remaining half of pastry to ⅛-inch thickness and place over filling. Trim edges of pastry; seal and flute edges. Cut slits to allow steam to escape; brush with egg white and sprinkle with remaining 1 tablespoon of sugar. Bake for 30 to 35 minutes.

Yield: 6 to 8 servings.

Strawberry Patch Shortcake

From March to May is peak strawberry time in the South. By far the most popular Southern strawberry dessert is strawberry shortcake. Nothing tastes better than a mouthful of this shortcake, juicy berries, and luscious whipped cream.

1 quart fresh strawberries, sliced
¼ cup sugar

Each bite of Slice o' Lemon Pie is filled with tart flavor. The secret to achieving the tart taste is to use more than just lemon juice; an entire lemon is sliced and stirred into the filling.

One key to great strawberry shortcake is letting the sliced berries stand in sugar for several hours before the cake is assembled. This will bring out the juice and make the berries extra sweet.

Shortcake:

2 cups all-purpose flour

¼ cup sugar

1 tablespoon baking powder

½ teaspoon salt

⅓ cup unsalted butter

¾ cup milk

1 egg

1 egg white

2 tablespoons sugar

Topping:

1 cup heavy cream

3 tablespoons sifted confectioners' sugar

Garnish:

Whole fresh strawberries

Combine sliced strawberries and ¼ cup sugar; stir gently. Cover and refrigerate 2 hours.

Lightly grease two 9-inch cake pans; set aside.

To make the shortcake dough, combine flour, sugar, baking powder, and salt in a large mixing bowl; cut in butter until mixture resembles coarse meal.

Preheat oven to 450° F.

Combine milk and egg; beat well. Add to flour mixture, stirring with a fork until a soft dough forms. Pat dough out evenly into cake pans (dough will be sticky, so moisten fingers with water).

Beat egg white until stiff peaks form. Brush surface of dough in each cake pan with beaten egg white. Sprinkle each layer with a tablespoon of sugar. Bake for 8 to 10 minutes or until golden brown. Remove shortcakes from pans and let cool completely on wire racks (layers will be thin).

To make topping, beat cream with an electric mixer on high speed until foamy; gradually add 3 tablespoons confectioners' sugar, beating until soft peaks form. Place 1 cake layer on serving plate. Spread half of whipped cream over layer and arrange half of sliced strawberries on top, using a slotted spoon. Repeat procedure with remaining cake layer, whipped cream (reserve a little for the garnish), and sliced strawberries. Garnish top of shortcake with the reserved whipped cream and whole strawberries.

Yield: 8 servings.

Praline Cheesecake

Cheesecake may not have originated in the South, but we know a good thing when we taste it. This is a wonderful recipe that I have made and served many times. In fact, I've had several dessert parties where I've served nothing but cheesecake and champagne.

Crust:

1¼ cups graham cracker crumbs

3 tablespoons brown sugar

¼ cup unsalted butter or margarine, melted

Filling:

3 (8-ounce) packages cream cheese, softened

1 cup firmly packed brown sugar

1 tablespoon all-purpose flour

3 eggs

1 teaspoon vanilla extract

1 teaspoon liquid butter flavoring

Topping:

1 (16-ounce) container sour cream

¼ cup brown sugar

½ teaspoon liquid butter flavoring

Garnish:

Chopped toasted pecans

Preheat oven to 350° F.

Make the crust by combining graham cracker crumbs, brown sugar, and butter; stir until well blended. Press crumb

Brown sugar laces the crust, the filling, and the topping of Praline Cheesecake to give it the flavor of buttery-sweet pralines from New Orleans.

mixture evenly over bottom and up sides of a 9-inch springform pan. Bake for 5 minutes. Let cool.

Raise oven temperature to 375° F.

To make the filling, beat cream cheese with an electric mixer on high speed until light and fluffy; gradually add brown sugar and flour, mixing well. Add eggs, one at a time, beating well after each addition. Stir in vanilla and butter flavoring. Pour mixture into prepared pan. Bake for 45 minutes, or until set. Remove from oven.

Raise oven temperature to 500° F.

To make the topping, combine sour cream, brown sugar, and butter flavoring; stir well. Spread sour cream mixture evenly over cheesecake. Bake for 5 minutes. Let cool to room temperature on a wire rack. Refrigerate cheesecake at least 8 hours before serving. Garnish with pecans.

Yield: 8 servings.

Mama's Banana Pudding

Banana pudding is widely enjoyed in the South. My mother always made her version of this dessert in a clear glass baking dish, so you could see the tempting layers of bananas, vanilla wafers, yellow pudding, and golden meringue.

½ cup sugar
3 tablespoons brown sugar
3 tablespoons cornstarch
¼ cup water
2 eggs, separated
1½ cups milk
1 teaspoon vanilla extract
20 to 25 vanilla wafers
2 medium bananas, sliced
⅛ teaspoon cream of tartar
2 tablespoons confectioners' sugar

Combine sugar, brown sugar, and cornstarch in a heavy saucepan, stirring well. Add ¼ cup water; mix well.

Beat egg yolks; add milk and mix well. Gradually stir milk mixture into sugar mixture. Cook over medium heat, stirring constantly, until mixture comes to a boil. Boil 1 minute, stirring constantly, until thickened. Remove from heat and stir in vanilla. Set aside to cool slightly.

Arrange half of vanilla wafers in the bottom of a 1½-quart baking dish; spread with half of pudding. Top with banana slices. Arrange remaining vanilla wafers around the outside edge of dish. Top with remaining pudding mixture.

Preheat oven to 325° F.

Combine egg whites and cream of tartar. Beat with an electric mixer on high speed until foamy. Gradually add confectioners' sugar, beating until stiff peaks form. Spread meringue over pudding, sealing to edge of dish. Bake for 20 minutes, or until golden brown.

Yield: 6 servings.

Leftover bananas on Saturday always meant my mother would make banana bread or banana pudding. I was quick to cast my vote for banana pudding because it was rich and sweet and topped with fluffy meringue. Through the years, many quicker versions of this favorite dessert have surfaced, but none of them are as tasty as the original.

Spring Menus
Memorable Occasions

*I*n the spring Easter touches hearts, old and young. Families renew their ties by gathering for Sunday dinner—usually roasted hen or sliced ham, vegetables, iced tea, and dessert. Several aunts will bring their favorite desserts, so there is a choice for every sweet tooth.

Afterward young girls and boys in pastel dresses and suits hunt gaily tinted eggs hidden in tufts of grass, wedged between rocks, and tucked between the protruding roots of trees. Soon hair bows fly and jackets are cast off. Shouts fill the air as the children uncover colorful treasures.

EASTER FAMILY LUNCH

Cream of Asparagus Soup

Arkansas Roasted Hen

Pasta-Rice Casserole

Caramelized Onions

Minted Sugar Snaps

Chocolate Roulage

Lemon Meringue Pie

Iced Tea

Cream of Asparagus Soup

I absolutely love cream soups. Here is my favorite way to savor the first tender spears of spring asparagus.

2 pounds fresh asparagus
2 tablespoons unsalted butter or
margarine
¼ cup minced onion
¼ cup chopped fresh parsley
1 teaspoon ground coriander
1 tablespoon all-purpose flour
2 cups chicken broth
1 cup half-and-half
2 teaspoons lemon juice
⅛ teaspoon white pepper

With the arrival of spring come the first thin spears of asparagus. Fresh asparagus is a treat simply steamed and topped with butter, but its full flavor really comes through when steamed and blended into Cream of Asparagus Soup. Each serving can be garnished with tender asparagus tips.

Snap off tough ends of asparagus. Cook asparagus, covered, in a small amount of boiling water for 10 minutes, or until fully tender. Cut off asparagus tips, reserving stalks. Set tips and stalks aside.

Melt the butter in a large saucepan; add onion, parsley, and coriander. Sauté over medium heat until onion is tender. Reduce heat to low and add flour; cook 1 minute, stirring constantly. Gradually add chicken broth; cook over medium heat, stirring constantly, for 5 minutes. Add reserved asparagus stalks.

Pour broth mixture into container of electric blender; process until smooth. Pour blended mixture into a heavy saucepan; stir in half-and-half and reserved asparagus tips. Add lemon juice and pepper; cook until heated through.

Yield: 4 servings.

Arkansas Roasted Hen

One of the most important crops in Arkansas is poultry. I once judged the Chicken Cooking Contest in Hot Springs and was surprised at all the imaginative recipes. It's hard to improve on the flavor of this simple roasted hen, however, a favorite throughout the South.

1 (4- to 6-pound) hen
Salt
⅓ cup unsalted butter or margarine,
    softened
1½ teaspoons chopped fresh marjoram
    or ½ teaspoon dried marjoram
¼ teaspoon hot sauce

Preheat oven to 375° F.
Remove giblets and neck from chicken; reserve for other uses. Rinse chicken with cold water and pat dry. Lift wing tips up and over the back so they are tucked under chicken. Sprinkle chicken cavities with salt. Close cavities and tie leg ends together with string; set aside.

Combine butter, marjoram, and hot sauce; spread over chicken. Sprinkle lightly with additional salt. Place chicken, breast side up, in a shallow roasting pan. Bake for 2 hours, or until drumsticks are easy to move up and down, basting often with pan drippings.

Yield: 4 servings.

Arkansas Roasted Hen, served on a bed of parsley and surrounded with Caramelized Onions, features the mild, sweet flavor of marjoram. The onions are steamed until tender, then baked in a sauce of butter, brown sugar, and corn syrup.

Pasta-Rice Casserole

Once in a while I discover a dish that has risen to local popularity because it tastes great and is easy to prepare. Here is my latest find.

⅓ cup unsalted butter or margarine
3 ounces spaghetti, broken into small
    pieces
1 cup regular long-grain rice,
    uncooked
1 teaspoon chicken-flavored bouillon
    granules
2 cups water
1¼ cups chicken or beef broth
⅓ cup chopped green onions
1 (8-ounce) can sliced water chestnuts,
    drained

Preheat oven to 350° F.

Melt butter in a large skillet. Add spaghetti; sauté over high heat until golden, stirring constantly. Remove from heat.

In a large bowl, combine sautéed spaghetti and rest of ingredients. Carefully pour into a lightly greased 8-inch-square baking dish. Bake, uncovered, for 40 to 50 minutes. Stir gently before serving.

Yield: 6 servings.

Pasta-Rice Casserole is flavored with chicken or beef broth and adds a nice texture to the menu. The casserole teams well with fresh sugar snaps tossed with red bell pepper, green onions, and mint.

Caramelized Onions

Southerners have always been fond of onions. We use them in salads, meat dishes, soups, casseroles, and breads. Here is a time-honored way to bake onions so that they cook up tender and sweet.

1 ½ pounds medium-size onions,
*   peeled*
¼ cup unsalted butter or margarine
½ cup firmly packed brown sugar
¼ cup light corn syrup
½ teaspoon salt

Arrange onions on a steaming rack. Place over boiling water; cover and steam 20 minutes, or until tender. Place in a lightly greased 8-inch-square baking dish.

Preheat oven to 350° F.

Melt butter in a saucepan over low heat. Add sugar, syrup, and salt and bring to a boil over medium heat. Reduce heat, and simmer 5 minutes. Pour glaze over onions; cover and bake for 25 to 30 minutes.

Yield: 4 to 6 servings.

Minted Sugar Snaps

Frozen peas, or even fresh market peas, never taste as good as the homegrown variety, which can be picked and rushed to the table within minutes. Sugar snaps have tender, edible pods, which means you can enjoy the whole pea and avoid hours of tedious shelling.

½ pound fresh sugar snap pea pods
2 tablespoons unsalted butter or
*   margarine*
1 large red bell pepper, cut into
*   ¼-inch strips*
3 tablespoons chopped green onions
1 tablespoon chopped fresh mint
¼ teaspoon salt

Wash sugar snaps and trim ends. Set aside.

Melt butter in a large skillet. Add sugar snaps and remaining ingredients and stir gently. Cover and cook over medium-high heat for 6 to 8 minutes, or until vegetables are crisp-tender. Serve immediately.

Yield: 4 servings.

Chocolate Roulage

This impressive dessert is actually easy to make. Don't worry if it cracks a bit when it is rolled up; just sprinkle on extra cocoa. It will look beautiful and taste great!

5 eggs, separated
1 cup sugar
6 tablespoons sifted cocoa
1 cup sifted cake flour
1 teaspoon unflavored gelatin
2 tablespoons cold water
1 ¼ cups heavy cream
3 tablespoons confectioners' sugar
½ teaspoon vanilla extract

Grease the bottom and sides of a 15- x 10- x 1-inch jelly-roll pan with vegetable oil and line with wax paper; grease and flour wax paper. Set pan aside.

Place egg yolks in a large bowl and beat with an electric mixer on high speed until foamy. Gradually add sugar, beating until mixture is thick and lemon-colored. Gradually stir in 3 tablespoons of the cocoa.

Preheat oven to 350° F.

Beat egg whites until stiff peaks form; fold into cocoa mixture. Gently fold cake flour into egg mixture. Spread batter evenly in prepared pan. Bake for 15 minutes.

Meanwhile, sift remaining cocoa onto a tea towel in a 15- x 10-inch rectangle. When cake is done, loosen from sides of pan and gently but quickly turn cake out onto towel. Peel off wax paper. Beginning at narrow end, roll up cake and towel. Place seam side down on a wire rack; let cool.

Sprinkle gelatin over 2 tablespoons cold water in a small saucepan; let stand 1 minute. Cook over low heat, stirring until gelatin dissolves. Beat cream with an electric mixer on low speed, gradually adding dissolved gelatin. Increase to medium speed and continue to beat until mixture begins to thicken. Add confectioners' sugar and vanilla; beat at high speed until soft peaks form.

Unroll cake and remove towel. Spread whipped cream mixture on cake, leaving a 1-inch margin around edges; reroll cake. Place on serving plate, seam side down.

Yield: 8 servings.

Chocolate Roulage features a delicate cocoa-flavored cake rolled around a filling of sweetened whipped cream. If you desire, the filled cake can be frozen and served later.

Lemon Meringue Pie

Lemon meringue pie must surely rank with pecan pie as one of the oldest and most popular pies in the South. This is a typical example of the luscious concoction, except that today it is suggested to cook meringues longer and at lower temperatures to be sure to avoid eating raw egg whites.

Single-Crust Pie Pastry (page 42)
1⅓ cups sugar
½ cup cornstarch
1¾ cups water
4 eggs, separated
3 tablespoons unsalted butter or
*   margarine*
1 tablespoon grated lemon rind
¼ cup lemon juice
½ teaspoon cream of tartar
¼ cup sifted confectioners' sugar

Preheat oven to 450° F.

Line a 9-inch pie plate with pastry; trim and flute edges. Bake for 12 to 14 minutes or until lightly browned. Let cool.

Combine sugar and cornstarch in a heavy saucepan. Gradually add 1¾ cups water, stirring until smooth. Cook over medium heat, stirring until mixture thickens and comes to a boil. Boil 1 minute, stirring constantly. Remove from heat.

Beat egg yolks with an electric mixer on high speed until thick and lemon-colored. Gradually stir about one-

All good Southern cooks seem to have a family recipe for Lemon Meringue Pie. When making this pie, be sure to add the lemon juice after the cornstarch-and-yolk mixture has thickened and is removed from the heat. If the juice is added before or during the cooking period, it will reduce the thickening ability of the cornstarch.

fourth of hot sugar mixture into beaten egg yolks; add egg yolks to remaining hot mixture, stirring constantly. Cook over medium heat, stirring for 2 to 3 minutes. Remove from heat. Add butter, lemon rind, and lemon juice; stir until butter melts. Spoon hot filling into baked pastry.

Lower oven temperature to 325° F.

Place egg whites and cream of tartar in a large bowl and beat with an electric mixer on high speed until foamy. Gradually add confectioners' sugar, 1 tablespoon at a time, beating until stiff peaks form and sugar dissolves. Immediately spread meringue over filling, sealing to edges of pastry. Bake for 25 to 30 minutes, or until top is browned and set, shielding edges of pastry with aluminum foil if pastry browns too quickly. Let pie cool several hours before slicing. Store pie in refrigerator.

Yield: 6 to 8 servings.

Teas and showers are still major social events in towns across the South. They are often held on Saturday or Sunday afternoon to honor a future bride or a soon-to-be mother. Refreshments are light—dainty sandwiches, cheese wafers, cookies, and punch.

It is not unusual for several hostesses to get together and share the cost of the party. When this is the case, they will often divide the menu, so that each prepares only a couple of recipes.

FANCY TEA OR SHOWER

Cucumber Tea Sandwiches

Chicken Salad in
Miniature Toast Cups

Decatur Cheese Wafers

Easy Jelly-Roll Swirl

Sweet Shower Mints

Sorghum Tea Cookies

Dainty Coffee Wafers

Champagne Punch

Hot Tea ◆ Coffee

Cucumber Tea Sandwiches

I think most Southern girls grow up eating these tiny sandwiches. They are the ultimate finger food and are served at all sorts of events, from tea parties for dolls to grown-up wedding showers and elaborate receptions.

> ½ small onion, coarsely chopped
> 2 (8-ounce) packages cream cheese, softened
> ½ teaspoon salt
> ¼ teaspoon ground white pepper
> 1 teaspoon minced fresh dillweed or ¼ teaspoon dried dillweed
> 80 slices thin white bread
> 1 large cucumber, peeled and thinly sliced

Garnish:

> 2 (3-ounce) packages cream cheese, softened
> 2 to 3 teaspoons milk
> Tiny sprigs of fresh dillweed (optional)

Place onion in container of food processor fitted with a metal blade and process until finely minced. Cut 2 (8-ounce) packages cream cheese into 1-inch pieces. Add to processor and process until smooth. Add salt, pepper, and dillweed; process until blended.

Cut bread slices into rounds, removing crusts, using a 2½-inch biscuit cutter. Spread about 1 tablespoon of the cream cheese mixture on 40 of the bread rounds. Arrange cucumber slices over cream cheese mixture. Top with remaining bread rounds.

Combine 2 (3-ounce) packages cream cheese and milk in a small bowl; mix until smooth. Spoon cream cheese mixture into a decorating bag fitted with a rosette tip; pipe a rosette of cream cheese on top of each sandwich. Garnish each sandwich with a sprig of dillweed.

Yield: 40 appetizer sandwiches.

Chicken Salad in Miniature Toast Cups

In order to entertain her bridge club or garden club, a good Southern hostess has to master the art of serving dainty portions of chicken salad. Even though this is a so-called party dish, the salad is also wonderful spread on slices of bread and turned into a sandwich.

1 loaf thinly sliced white bread
Unsalted butter or margarine, softened
1 cup finely chopped cooked chicken
½ cup finely minced celery
¼ cup finely chopped pecans, toasted
1 teaspoon honey mustard
1 teaspoon lemon juice
Mayonnaise
Salt and black pepper to taste

Preheat oven to 325° F.

Roll bread slices flat with a rolling pin. Lightly butter one side of each slice of bread. Cut each slice into four 2-inch rounds, removing crusts, using a small cookie or biscuit cutter. Press rounds into miniature muffin tins, buttered side up. Bake for 10 to 15 minutes, or until lightly browned. Remove from tins and cool completely.

Combine chicken, celery, pecans, honey mustard, and lemon juice, stirring gently. Add enough mayonnaise to moisten chicken mixture. Season with salt and pepper. Fill toast cups.

Yield: 70 filled toast cups.

Each tiny Cucumber Tea Sandwich is filled with a thin slice of cucumber and garnished with a rosette of cream cheese and a sprig of fresh dill. Chicken Salad in Miniature Toast Cups is an elegant way to serve bite-size portions of crunchy chicken salad.

Decatur Cheese Wafers

Up around Decatur, Alabama, a social gathering just isn't complete without a tray of cheese wafers. These little rounds taste very similar to cheese straws. And the red pepper gives them a nice warm bite.

    2 cups (8 ounces) shredded sharp
       Cheddar cheese, softened
½ cup unsalted butter, softened
1¾ cups all-purpose flour
¾ teaspoon cayenne pepper
⅛ teaspoon salt
Pecan halves

Combine cheese, butter, flour, cayenne, and salt; mix until blended. Shape dough into two long rolls; wrap in wax paper and chill at least 3 hours.

Preheat oven to 350° F.

Unwrap rolls and cut into ¼-inch slices; place on ungreased baking sheets. Mash a pecan half in center of each wafer. Bake for 12 to 15 minutes, or until lightly browned. Cool on wire racks.

Yield: 4 to 5 dozen.

Easy Jelly-Roll Swirl

This simple rolled cake is filled with jelly, but you might also fill it with whipped cream. Rather than being frosted, the cake is sprinkled with confectioners' sugar.

    4 eggs
¾ teaspoon baking powder
½ teaspoon salt
1 cup sugar
1 cup all-purpose flour
1 teaspoon vanilla extract
Confectioners' sugar
1 cup raspberry or strawberry jelly

Grease a 15- x 10- x 1-inch jelly-roll pan and line with wax paper; grease and flour wax paper. Set aside.

Preheat oven to 400° F.

Combine eggs, baking powder, and salt; beat with electric mixer on high speed until foamy. Gradually add sugar, beating until thick and lemon-colored. Fold in flour and vanilla extract. Spread batter evenly in prepared pan. Bake for 10 to 12 minutes, or until top of cake springs back when touched.

Sift the confectioners' sugar in a 15- x 10-inch rectangle on a tea towel.

A takeoff on traditional cheese straws, Decatur Cheese Wafers are a crisp blend of Cheddar cheese, pecans, and cayenne. Be sure to chill the wafer dough before slicing, for much neater handling.

No shower or tea should be without at least one fancy cake or dessert. Even though Easy Jelly-Roll Swirl looks fancy, it is just as its name implies—a simple rolled cake filled with sweet jelly and sprinkled with powdered sugar.

When cake is done, immediately loosen from sides of pan and turn out onto sugar. Peel off wax paper. Roll cake and towel up together (sideways for a short, thick cake, or lengthwise for a long, thin cake). Cool cake rolled in towel, seam side down, for about 15 minutes.

Unroll cake; remove towel. Spread cake with jelly and reroll. Place on serving plate, seam side down. Cool completely.

Yield: 10 servings.

Sweet Shower Mints are standard fare at teas, showers, and receptions. These dainty sweets are very easy to make using rubber candy molds, and they can be tinted to match most color schemes.

Sweet Shower Mints

These tiny melt-in-your-mouth mints show up at most bridal showers and receptions. I expect they have gained lasting popularity not only because they are easy to make but also because they look pretty with pastel color schemes.

1 (16-ounce) package confectioners'
*   sugar, sifted*
½ cup unsalted butter, softened
2 tablespoons heavy cream
4 drops peppermint or almond extract
2 to 4 drops liquid food coloring

Combine sugar, butter, cream, and extract in a large mixing bowl; beat with an electric mixer on high speed just until blended. Gradually add liquid food coloring until mixture reaches desired color, blending well.

Knead candy mixture until smooth. Press into rubber candy molds and cover with paper towels; let stand overnight or until dry and firm. Remove candy from molds and store in an airtight container.

Yield: 4 dozen.

Sorghum Tea Cookies

During the War Between the States, when sugar was difficult to come by, sorghum became a common sugar substitute. Sorghum grows in stalks that, like sugar cane, yield a juice when pressed. The juice is boiled down to make a syrup called sorghum syrup.

> *1 cup unsalted butter, softened*
> *¾ cup sugar*
> *3 eggs*
> *1 cup sorghum syrup*
> *2 tablespoons buttermilk*
> *6 to 7 cups all-purpose flour*
> *1 teaspoon baking soda*
> *2 teaspoons ground cinnamon*
> *Additional sugar for sprinkling*

Cream butter with an electric mixer on low speed; gradually add sugar, beating on medium speed until light and fluffy. Add eggs, one at a time, beating well after each addition. Add sorghum syrup and buttermilk. Mix well.

Combine flour, soda, and cinnamon. Stir dry ingredients into creamed mixture. Cover dough and refrigerate overnight.

Preheat oven to 375° F.

Roll dough out to ¼-inch thickness on a lightly floured board; cut with a 1½-inch cookie cutter. Place cookies on a lightly greased baking sheet. Sprinkle lightly with sugar. Bake for 8 to 10 minutes, or until golden brown; cool on wire racks.

Yield: 8 to 9 dozen.

Dainty Coffee Wafers

These delicate cookies are a modern invention, made with a cookie press. Serve them up at your next tea or shower and you will be rewarded with smiles of delight.

> *¼ cup plus 2 tablespoons unsalted*
> *butter or margarine, softened*
> *½ cup sugar*

Sorghum Tea Cookies are made from a rich dough that is refrigerated overnight, then rolled and cut into shapes with cookie cutters. The dough for Dainty Coffee Wafers is pressed from a cookie press into ribbonlike strips.

2 tablespoons milk
2 tablespoons instant coffee granules
1 egg
½ teaspoon vanilla extract
2¼ cups all-purpose flour
1 teaspoon ground cinnamon

Preheat oven to 400° F.

Cream butter with an electric mixer on low speed; gradually add sugar, beating at medium speed until light and fluffy. Combine milk and coffee granules, stirring well. Add coffee mixture, egg, and vanilla to creamed mixture, beating well.

Combine flour and cinnamon; add to creamed mixture, mixing well.

Press dough from a cookie press onto ungreased baking sheets, making 2-inch ribbonlike strips. Bake for 6 minutes, or until edges are lightly browned. Remove from baking sheets and let cool completely on wire racks.

Yield: about 5 dozen.

Champagne Punch

This punch recipe has proved popular over the years. It is a refreshing blend of citrus juice and champagne; add a little grenadine or cherry juice for a pretty pink color.

2 (6-ounce) cans frozen orange juice
    concentrate, thawed and undiluted
2 (6-ounce) cans frozen lemonade
    concentrate, thawed and undiluted
1 (1-quart) bottle tonic water
Ice cubes or ice ring
1 (1-liter) bottle ginger ale, chilled
1 (750-milliliter) bottle champagne,
    chilled
½ cup grenadine or maraschino cherry
    juice (optional)

Combine orange juice concentrate, lemonade concentrate, and tonic water; chill well. Pour mixture over ice in a large punch bowl. Gently stir in ginger ale and champagne. Add grenadine or cherry juice if a pink color is desired.

Yield: about 3½ quarts.

Make an attractive ice ring for Champagne Punch by arranging lemon, lime, and orange slices in your favorite gelatin mold; fill the mold with water or orange juice and freeze. Before serving, unmold the ice ring and set it into the punch bowl; then fill the bowl with punch.

The horses have "run for the roses" in Louisville, Kentucky, since 1875. Well past its centennial, the Derby is still off and running the first Saturday of every May. All across the South, but especially in Kentucky, there are dinners, lunches, and brunches in honor of this occasion. Party conversation focuses intensely on the upcoming race unless guests are temporarily distracted by country ham, fresh strawberries, and mint juleps.

DERBY DAY BRUNCH

Citrus Burst Fruit Dip

Spring Spinach Salad

Brunch Eggs

Roast Smithfield Country Ham

Modern Beaten Biscuits

Marinated Asparagus Spears

Derby Pecan Tarts

Mint Juleps

Citrus Burst Fruit Dip

This sweet dip is ideal for serving with fresh fruit—perhaps strawberries, pineapple chunks, banana slices, and grapes. If attractively arranged on a pretty tray, the fruit and dip will look impressive enough to form the centerpiece of your party table.

1 (8-ounce) package cream cheese, softened
1 (7-ounce) jar marshmallow creme
1 tablespoon grated orange rind
1 tablespoon grated lemon rind
2 tablespoons orange juice
2 tablespoons lemon juice
½ teaspoon ground ginger

Garnish:
Sprigs of fresh mint

Citrus Burst Fruit Dip can be offered from a silver bowl and surrounded by strawberries, fresh pineapple, banana chunks, and green grapes for dipping.

Beat cream cheese with an electric mixer on low speed until smooth. Stir in rest of ingredients and beat mixture until smooth. Transfer to a bowl and garnish with fresh mint.

Yield: 1½ cups.

Spring Spinach Salad

A "mess" of fresh, tender spinach makes a lovely salad. Here the leaves are combined with spring strawberries and dressed with a mixture of oil and vinegar.

1 pound fresh tender spinach leaves
1 pint fresh strawberries, washed, hulled, and halved

Vinaigrette:
½ cup sugar
2 tablespoons sesame seeds, toasted
1½ teaspoons grated onion
¼ teaspoon Worcestershire sauce
¼ teaspoon paprika
½ cup vegetable oil
¼ cup cider vinegar or strawberry vinegar

Remove stems from spinach leaves and wash leaves thoroughly. Pat dry and tear into bite-size pieces. Combine spinach and strawberries in a large bowl, tossing gently.

Combine vinaigrette ingredients in

Tender spring spinach leaves and tart fresh strawberries are tossed with a tangy vinaigrette dressing for Spring Spinach Salad.

container of an electric blender; cover and process at low speed for 30 seconds. Drizzle dressing over salad; toss gently.

Yield: 4 to 6 servings.

Brunch Eggs

This delicious casserole of scrambled eggs has become a classic brunch dish. One reason for its popularity is that it can be made the day ahead and refrigerated. Slip it in the oven to bake 30 minutes before you are ready to serve.

2 tablespoons unsalted butter or
*   margarine*
2½ tablespoons all-purpose flour
2 cups milk
1 cup (4 ounces) shredded Cheddar
*   cheese*
⅛ teaspoon hot sauce
5 slices bacon
½ cup diced ham

¼ cup chopped green onions
12 eggs, beaten
1 (4-ounce) can sliced mushrooms,
*   drained*
⅔ cup soft fresh bread crumbs
¼ teaspoon paprika

Melt butter in a heavy saucepan over low heat; add flour, stirring until smooth. Cook 1 minute, stirring constantly. Gradually add milk; cook over medium heat, stirring constantly, until thickened and bubbly. Add cheese and hot sauce; stir until cheese melts and mixture is smooth. Set cheese sauce mixture aside.

Cook bacon in a large skillet until crisp; remove bacon, reserving 3 tablespoons drippings in skillet. Crumble bacon and set aside. Sauté ham and green onions in drippings until tender; add eggs and crumbled bacon. Cook without stirring until mixture begins to set on bottom, then stir gently to form large, soft curds. When eggs are set, stir in mushrooms and cheese sauce. Spoon egg mixture into a lightly greased 12- x 8- x 2-inch baking dish. Combine bread crumbs and paprika, stirring well. Sprinkle over egg mixture. Cover and refrigerate 8 hours.

Preheat oven to 350° F.

Remove casserole from refrigerator; bake, uncovered, for 30 minutes, or until heated through.

Yield: 6 to 8 servings.

Roast Smithfield Country Ham

Smithfield, Virginia, reigns as the most famous producer of country hams. In fact, a "genuine Smithfield ham" can be produced only within the city limits of Smithfield, Virginia. These hams are characterized by a long-cut shank and seasonings of apple, oak, and hickory smoke.

1 (12- to 14-pound) uncooked
    Smithfield country ham
1 quart apple cider
2 cups apple juice
2 cups orange juice
Whole cloves
2 cups firmly packed brown sugar
2 tablespoons water

Place ham in a very large container; cover with water and soak 24 hours to remove excess salt. Pour off water. Scrub ham in warm water with a stiff brush and rinse well.

Preheat oven to 325° F.

Drain ham; place in a large roasting pan and cover with apple cider, apple juice, and orange juice. Insert a meat thermometer into ham, making sure it does not touch fat or bone. Cover and bake, basting with pan juices, for 2½ to 3 hours, or until meat thermometer registers 142° F. (about 15 minutes per pound). Drain ham and let cool. Discard pan juices.

Place ham fat side up on a cutting board; remove skin from ham and score fat in a diamond design. Stud with cloves. Return ham to roaster, fat side up. Pat 1½ cups of the brown sugar over ham. Combine remaining brown sugar and 2 tablespoons water in a small saucepan; place over low heat, stirring until sugar is melted. Brush ham with sugar glaze. Place ham on lowest rack in oven and roast 5 minutes, basting with sugar glaze.

Remove ham from roaster and carve into thin slices.

Yield: 25 to 35 servings.

Modern Beaten Biscuits

True beaten biscuits have all but disappeared in the South. One reason is that they require so much time and effort to make. For example, some old recipes suggested that the dough be beaten vigorously at least 200 times. The version below has been adapted to make use of the convenient food processor.

2 cups all-purpose flour
1 teaspoon sugar
½ teaspoon salt
½ teaspoon baking powder
½ cup cold solid vegetable shortening
¼ cup half-and-half
¼ cup ice water

Place flour, sugar, salt, and baking powder in a food processor fitted with a metal blade. Cover and process 1 second to mix. Add shortening; cover and process 5 to 6 seconds, or until mixture resembles coarse meal.

With the food processor running, add the half-and-half and ice water in a stream through the food chute. Process until dough forms a ball. Continue processing 2 additional minutes.

Preheat oven to 350° F.

Turn dough out onto a lightly floured board. Roll dough out to ¼-inch thickness; fold dough over on itself to make 2 layers. Cut dough with a 1¾-inch biscuit cutter. Place on an ungreased baking sheet; prick each biscuit 2 or 3 times with the tines of a fork. Bake for 30 minutes, or until biscuits are lightly browned.

Yield: about 2 dozen.

The first step in making Roast Smithfield Country Ham is to soak the ham in water for 24 hours; then pour off the water, scrub the ham with a brush, and rinse well. This procedure will help remove any excess saltiness. Paper-thin slivers of ham team perfectly with Modern Beaten Biscuits.

Marinated Asparagus Spears

Asparagus is a beautiful vegetable, but it requires patience and attention to grow. After waiting three years, my husband and I are expecting our first good asparagus harvest. Here is a simple recipe that makes this vegetable easy to serve.

1 pound fresh, thin asparagus spears

Marinade:
¼ cup cider vinegar
¼ cup vegetable oil
½ teaspoon salt
¼ teaspoon white pepper
¼ teaspoon garlic powder
2 tablespoons diced pimiento
1 tablespoon minced fresh parsley

Snap off tough ends of asparagus. Cook asparagus, covered, in boiling water for 6 minutes, or until crisp-tender. Drain well and arrange spears in a shallow dish.

Combine marinade ingredients, stirring well. Pour dressing over asparagus; cover, and refrigerate overnight. Serve asparagus over shredded lettuce or with a slotted spoon.

Yield: 4 servings.

Derby Pecan Tarts are like miniature pecan pies. For best results, chill the cream cheese dough for an hour before shaping in miniature muffin pans.

Derby Pecan Tarts

There are many traditions associated with the Kentucky Derby. One of them is serving these tarts at pre-race parties.

Tart-Pastry Shells:
1 (3-ounce) package cream cheese, softened
½ cup unsalted butter, softened
1 cup all-purpose flour

Filling:
¾ cup firmly packed brown sugar
1 teaspoon unsalted butter, softened
1 egg
¼ teaspoon salt
1 teaspoon vanilla extract
¾ cup chopped pecans

Combine cream cheese and butter; blend by hand until smooth. Add flour,

Marinated Asparagus Spears are a colorful addition to spring menus. The thin spears are cooked just until crisp-tender, then soaked overnight in a tangy marinade.

mixing well. Refrigerate dough for 1 hour.

Preheat oven to 350° F.

Shape dough into 24 balls; place each in a lightly greased miniature muffin pan, pressing with fingers to form a shell. Bake for 15 minutes, or until lightly browned. Let tart shells cool before filling.

Combine ingredients for filling, mixing well. Spoon 1 teaspoon of filling into each pastry shell. Bake for 15 minutes or until golden and set.

Yield: 2 dozen tarts.

Place 1 cup lightly packed mint sprigs in a heavy saucepan; crush mint with fingers or bruise with the back of a spoon. Add 1½ cups water to saucepan; bring mixture to a boil. Cook, covered, 5 minutes. Add sugar, stirring well; return to a boil. Cover, reduce heat, and simmer 5 minutes. Let syrup cool. Place mint syrup in a small bowl or jar; cover and let stand 4 to 6 hours. Strain mixture, discarding mint and saving syrup.

To serve, fill each julep cup or small glass with 1 cup crushed ice. Add 1 tablespoon syrup and ¼ cup bourbon for each serving, stirring gently. Garnish with sprigs of fresh mint.

Yield: 24 servings.

Mint Juleps

I will never forget the first time I sampled a mint julep. I expected a dainty, frivolous concoction, but it took only one sip to put those thoughts to rest. In the South, mint juleps are most often served in frosty silver mint julep cups.

1 cup lightly packed fresh mint sprigs
1½ cups water
1 cup sugar
1½ gallons crushed ice
1½ quarts bourbon

Garnish:
Sprigs of fresh mint

The sugar-mint syrup for Mint Juleps can be made ahead and refrigerated. For the perfect drink, fill each silver julep cup with crushed ice before adding the syrup and bourbon; garnish with a spring of fresh mint.

Summer

Catching a Breeze

Summer begins as humid air
descends and trees no longer rustle in the breeze.
Vegetables and herbs are in the garden, and fat bouquets of
flowers fill the house. Neighbors visit in porch rocking
chairs as they fan themselves and listen
to the katydids sing.

Left: Spanish moss hangs like pendants in the swampy marsh areas near Saint Simons Island, Georgia.
♦ Center: The ponderous arms of this ancient live oak at Middleton Place, near Charleston, suffered from the
fury of Hurricane Hugo. The survival of the tree is essential, especially when we consider that it is part of the

The days move slowly, as heat settles in for the summer. On the coast, especially near bays, afternoon showers break the sun's hot grip. Steam rises off the street, as if drifting from a hot bathtub.

To cool off, we move out of the house and onto porches for quiet mornings and evenings. We sip from tall glasses of iced tea or lemonade as we survey the flowers, blooming their boldest in

earliest known landscaped garden in America. ♦ Right: The immensity of the sea and sky is never more apparent than in the late evening. At the end of a blistering-hot day, the sand becomes cool and damp, and the sea grasses dip gently in the breezes blowing off the water.

the bright sun. Oaks and elms, anchored for generations, protectively shade children while they play.

Vegetable gardens, which began spring wearing delicate shades of green, burst almost overnight with offerings. Squash peep from their orange-yellow blooms, beans hang from the vine, and cucumbers seem to grow inches every day. Tomatoes begin to redden, and mouths begin to

Right: All Saints Parish on Pawleys Island is one of the oldest churches in the state of South Carolina. The church is situated on the edge of a lush marshland. ✦ Below: Emerald Isle, North Carolina, is approximately 30 miles long; the ocean side is lined with vacation homes and graceful sea oats.

water in anticipation of tasting the first ripe ones, still warm from the sun.

As the summer drags on, the kitchen gears up to can and preserve the excess bounty. Kettles and boiling-water baths are readied for making pickles, jellies, and preserves. Berry patches, studded with strawberries, blueberries, and blackberries, are combed for their treasures. Peach orchards glisten with ripe fruit waiting to be made into cobblers and pies.

Escaping to the lake or seaside is the ultimate treat. Many families plan vacations at a certain time and place, year in and year out. Sometimes three generations will spend a week or two at their favorite weatherbeaten cottage or sleek condominium for a laid-back reunion of swimming, fishing, sailing, and visiting.

Right: Beach grasses top sand dunes on Pawleys Island, off the coast of South Carolina. Established dunes help protect the rest of the island from erosion. ✦ *Below and below right: Each year when the temperature begins to rise and the sky turns clean and blue, we Southerners head to the beach. With the ceremonial planting of the beach umbrella, lounge chairs are lined up for the best view of the waves and passing sunbathers.*

No one minds the heat in such a setting, for a breeze always blows, and umbrellas splashed with cheerful colors offer a haven when the sun blazes. Long walks by the water's edge refresh, with waves lapping at bare feet.

By evening, after a long day of swimming and dozing in the sun, everyone is hungry. Family members gather on the deck to peel boiled shrimp and shell crabs for dinner. Sometimes ears of corn, potatoes, crabs, and shrimp are tossed together in one great pot for a seafood boil.

Sizzling steaks, hamburgers, and hot dogs on Memorial Day herald weeks of tantalizing fish fries and picnics capped off by Fourth of July and Labor Day celebrations.

Summer's Respite

During the hot summer months Southerners seem to have one main thought on their minds—escaping the oppressive heat. In the days before air-conditioning, it would have been difficult to survive the summer in a house without a porch. On extremely hot days, meals were even eaten on the porch. Sometimes plates were filled in the kitchen and taken outside, where everyone would sit on the steps or in rocking chairs. Other times the kitchen

Opposite: Spanish moss is a common sight near Southern seacoasts. It is not unusual to see this silver-gray air plant hanging from trees, telephone lines, and fences. ♦ Inset: Even today the porches of many small-town Southern homes are lined with rocking chairs—evidence that rocking continues to be a favorite activity. In Beaufort, North Carolina, these cushioned chairs beckon evening rockers. ♦ Above: Summer is the time to seek solace from busy work schedules by spending relaxing afternoons with families and friends at the beach or on the river. As the hot afternoon sun begins to settle behind leafy trees, we might launch a small fishing boat on the rippling water of a favorite lake. Soft voices, discussing which type of bait to use, float across the water's surface, and echo from the shore. Southern fishermen can think of no better way to enjoy the season.

table was moved to the porch in June, where it would stay until September. The table also made a cooler workplace whenever there were peas to shell, ears of corn to shuck, or peaches to peel.

Early in the morning or in the evening after dinner, folks would visit quietly on the porch and watch children play in the yard. The slow back-and-forth movement of worn rocking chairs was both soothing and cooling.

It is hard to imagine summer in the South without porches. But it is even harder to imagine our landscape without the benefit of shade trees. They cool us from summer to summer; they provide a place for children to climb and build forts, a backdrop for weddings and picnics.

If it is impossible to find a cool spot beneath a shade tree, then a trip to the beach is a good alternative. From sunrise to sunset, and on into the night, Southerners walk the breezy beaches of the Gulf and the Atlantic. They sit for hours each day in a folding chair at the edge of the water, allowing the tide to ripple around their feet.

When we can't make it to the beach, we aim for the cool waters of a river or lake for more warm-weather activities. The dark, flowing waters of the Mis-

Left and above left: The popularity of the porch reached an all-time high during the last half of the nineteenth century, when Victorian architectural styles became a craze. These gingerbread-trimmed porches were designed to be both decorative and functional. Not only were the porches lovely, they also provided a natural place for sitting and communicating—they allowed you to see and be seen.

The Chattahoochee River is 436 miles long and forms the southern part of the boundary between Alabama and Georgia. The river flows south to the Apalachicola River, in northwest Florida, and eventually connects to the Gulf of Mexico.

sissippi, the Chattahoochee, the Tennessee, and the Suwannee have inspired poetry and songs and have been enjoyed by many Southerners who have taken fishing or boating vacations there. Some adventuresome souls like to raft down the famed Ocoee River in the Cherokee National Forest or the Nantahala River near the Smoky Mountains of Tennessee. But most of us prefer something tamer—like swimming or fishing at the lake.

We Southerners grow up learning to fish for bream, bass, crappie, and catfish. We start out with a cane pole and later learn to cast with a rod and reel. As skills mature we move on to fly fishing in cold mountain streams. We learn to fish, and we also learn the pleasure of cooking our catch. Wonderful memories of sharing fried fish, coleslaw, and hush puppies with our families on warm summer evenings are etched in our minds forever.

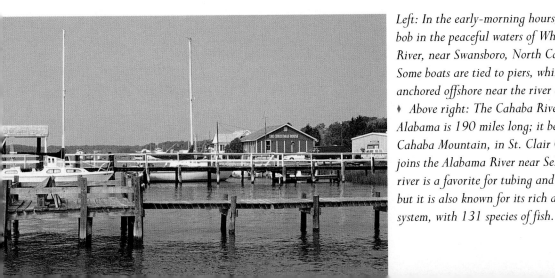

Left: In the early-morning hours, sailboats bob in the peaceful waters of White Oak River, near Swansboro, North Carolina. Some boats are tied to piers, while others are anchored offshore near the river channel.
♦ Above right: The Cahaba River in Alabama is 190 miles long; it begins on Cahaba Mountain, in St. Clair County, and joins the Alabama River near Selma. The river is a favorite for tubing and canoeing, but it is also known for its rich aquatic system, with 131 species of fish.

Glorious Bounty

The bounty that begins to appear in spring comes to full fruition in summer. Gardens and fields explode into brilliant colors. The lengthening evenings allow extra time for weeding, hoeing, and watering.

Summer in the South is neither fragile nor tentative. White-petaled daisies confidently burst into view. Coneflowers, each stem sporting a purple sun hat, soon follow. Tall hollyhocks, foxgloves, yarrow, and sunflowers bank yards with summer color. Roses are tended with loving care. Hydrangeas, tinted blue, pink,

Opposite: Coneflowers resist drought and bloom prolifically. The most popular selections are pink, purple, or white with maroon or bronze centers. ♦ Inset: Summer is a good time to venture off Southern interstates, for this is when roadside stands pop up along country roads. Its not unusual to see farmers offering their finest produce from the backs of pickup trucks, while others sell from small sheds or lean-tos. Tempting signs entice the curious to stop and admire baskets filled with fresh fruits and vegetables. ♦ Above: Summer in the South brings a predictable weather pattern of hot days and afternoon showers. When the growing season goes well, this South Carolina field of sunflowers pushes up tall and strong.

The crepe myrtle is the premier small tree of summer; it is adaptable to rugged conditions and offers unsurpassed color selections—from whites and pinks to reds and lavenders. While it is not necessary to prune a crepe myrtle, tip pruning (removing the flower clusters after blooming) does encourage blooming the following season. Pruning beneath the flower canopy to remove twiggy growth will give the tree a cleaner appearance and increase its sculptural character.

or white, add a fullness and softness to the garden. And crepe myrtles suddenly become beautiful in their pink and fuchsia summer gowns.

Anyone driving through the countryside will pass fields of dazzling white cotton and tall green cornstalks. Spontaneous markets created by farmers who park trucks at intersections begin to appear along the roads. Sometimes a rural family will set up a market in the front yard, complete with signs advertising the local specialty. Near the coasts, fishermen selling shrimp and crawfish may set up shop beside a truckload of watermelons and cantaloupe.

Sometimes vegetables are sold in "curb markets," semiperma-

Cotton flowering usually starts in the summer and lasts until the first autumn frost. The boll, which contains the cotton fibers, begins to form while the flower withers. The boll grows to about the size of a golf ball, then splits open, revealing four or five "locks" of fluffed-out cotton. Picking was done by hand until the 1960s, but today cotton is often harvested by stripping machines. The machines have already pulled off most of the bolls and leaves found in this Mississippi cotton field.

nent, open-sided structures located where it is easy to stop the car and hop out to sort through the colorful displays. In the city the farmers' market, which often retains the open-air atmosphere of smaller markets, draws lots of shoppers. These markets carry us back to the days when every courthouse square would be surrounded by vegetable dealers on market days.

The star of summer gardens is always the tomato. Most everyone with a small plot of land sets out at least a few tomato plants each year. As the vines become laden, familiar recipes for fried green tomatoes, tomato salad, tomato soup, and tomato aspic are prepared once again.

Across the lower South, summer brings a bounty of figs. In June and July, the sweet fruit crowds the branches of orchards and backyard trees. Homemakers love to turn this summer fruit into preserves, cakes, and cobblers.

And nothing says "Summer!" like a juicy slice of ice-cold watermelon. The favorite way to eat watermelon is just sliced on a plate or split open on a picnic table. But some cooks like to cut the juicy fruit into chunks or tiny round balls for cold salads. There are even those who save the rind for sweet watermelon-rind pickles.

Top right: Tourists traveling on U.S. 231 will almost always slow down or stop in Cottondale, Florida, to view the many produce stands lining both sides of the shady highway. The colorful stands beckon travelers to take home a bag of Florida oranges, vine-ripened tomatoes, Georgia Vidalia onions, or boiled peanuts. ♦ Center: To select a ripe watermelon, look for one that is symmetrically shaped and has a dull, velvety rind. The underside should be turning from white or pale green to a light yellowish color. ♦ Right: Brown turkey and Celeste are the most popular fig selections in the South. A fig is ripe when it becomes plump, turns brown or purple, and begins to droop. Ripe figs will not keep, so they need to be eaten fresh or cooked right away.

Summer Recipes
A Taste for Fun

CONDIMENTS

When the summer garden reaches its peak, Southern cooks know that it is time to restock the pantry with homemade pickles, jams, preserves, and marmalades. For about a week there is a frenzy of chopping, cutting, peeling, and mashing going on in the kitchen. Kettles and boiling-water baths are taken out of storage. The aroma of boiling vinegar, sugar, and spices drifts through the air. Afterward, as jars cool and lids pop and seal, cooks beam with a sense of accomplishment in the knowledge that their families will enjoy the fruits of their efforts all year long.

Sweet Pickled Peaches

My grandmother always served pickled peaches for Sunday dinner. Sometimes she would serve the peaches unadorned on a plate by themselves; other times she would use them as a garnish, along with parsley, for a large ham.

30 to 35 small, firm, ripe peaches
3 quarts cold water
1 teaspoon ascorbic-citric powder
6 (4-inch) sticks cinnamon
3 tablespoons whole cloves
5½ cups sugar
3 cups cider vinegar (5% acidity)

Peel peaches by preparing a saucepan of boiling water; dip each peach into water for 30 seconds. Pull off and discard skins.

To prevent peaches from turning dark, combine 3 quarts cold water and ascorbic-citric powder in a large container. Drop peeled peaches into water mixture; set aside.

Tie cinnamon sticks and cloves together in a cheesecloth bag. Combine spice bag, 4½ cups of the sugar, the vinegar, and 2 cups water in a large Dutch oven; bring to a full rolling boil. Let boil 3 minutes, stirring occasionally, until sugar dissolves.

Drain peaches. Add peaches to mixture in Dutch oven; reduce heat and simmer 2 minutes, or until peaches are heated through. Remove from heat; cover and let stand overnight.

When gardeners are faced with the dilemma of excess produce, they usually turn to canning and preserving. Several days each summer might be devoted to making Sweet Pickled Peaches, Yellow Squash Pickles, and Pepper Jelly.

Place Dutch oven over medium heat. Heat peaches thoroughly in syrup mixture. Pack hot peaches into hot sterilized jars. Add remaining 1 cup sugar to syrup mixture in Dutch oven; bring to a boil. Remove and discard cheesecloth bag; pour boiling syrup over peaches in jars, leaving ½-inch headspace. Remove air bubbles; wipe jar rims. Cover at once with metal lids and screw on bands. Process in boiling-water bath for 20 minutes.

Yield: 3 quarts.

Pepper Jelly

Pepper jelly has recently enjoyed a new surge of popularity. This sweet-hot jelly makes a delicious appetizer when spooned over cream cheese and spread over crackers. Some folks like to put up a few jars of green- or red-tinted jelly for the Christmas holidays.

1 ¼ cups minced green bell pepper
½ cup minced hot green chili pepper
7 ¼ cups sugar
1 ½ cups cider vinegar (5% acidity)
2 (3-ounce) packages liquid pectin
Green or red food coloring (optional)

Combine peppers, sugar, and vinegar in a Dutch oven; bring to a boil. Boil 5 minutes, stirring frequently. Add pectin and several drops of food coloring, if desired, and bring to a full rolling boil. Boil 1 minute, stirring frequently. Remove from heat and skim off foam with a metal spoon.

Quickly pour hot jelly into hot sterilized jars, leaving ¼-inch headspace; wipe jar rims. Cover at once with metal lids and screw on bands. Process in boiling-water bath for 5 minutes.

Yield: 6 half pints or 12 quarter pints.

Figs are grown in backyards all over the Deep South. It is fun to eat peeled figs with vanilla ice cream, but I think this fruit is at its best cooked into sweet preserves and spread over a hot biscuit.

Daddy's Favorite Fig Preserves

Each summer the fig tree next to my father's garden becomes loaded with juicy figs. This is when my mother cooks up her magical fig preserves. The ingredient list is simple, but friends and family have become addicted to the sweet, syrupy preserves and expect to receive at least one pint as a gift.

5 quarts ripe fresh figs
5 cups sugar

Wash figs several times, removing and discarding stems. Place figs in a large Dutch oven or kettle. Cover with sugar; let stand overnight (liquid will drain from figs).

Cook fig mixture over low heat for 2 to 3 hours (cooking time will vary according to ripeness of figs), stirring occasionally, until most of the liquid has evaporated and mixture thickens (some figs will fall apart).

Spoon figs into hot sterilized jars, leaving ¼-inch headspace. Remove air bubbles; wipe jar rims. Cover at once with metal lids and screw on bands. Process in boiling-water bath for 10 minutes.

Yield: 5 pints.

Yellow Squash Pickles

Southerners have long prided themselves on their pickled foods, and this bright yellow pickle happens to be one of the best. It is a terrific way to enjoy summer squash all year long.

16 cups sliced small yellow squash
1½ large onions, sliced
1 small red bell pepper, chopped
¾ cup salt
3¾ cups sugar
2¼ cups white vinegar (5% acidity)
¼ cup pickling salt
2 teaspoons celery seeds
2 teaspoons mustard seeds
2 teaspoons ground turmeric

Combine squash, onion, and pepper in a large bowl; sprinkle with the salt. Cover and let stand 2 hours. Rinse vegetables several times in cold water; drain well.

Combine remaining ingredients in a medium saucepan; bring to a boil. Cook, stirring constantly, until sugar dissolves.

Pack vegetables into hot sterilized jars; cover with hot syrup, leaving ½-inch headspace. Remove air bubbles; wipe jar rims. Cover at once with metal lids and screw on bands. Process in boiling-water bath for 15 minutes.

Yield: 7 pints.

Commercial fishing establish- ments dot the creeks and inlets of Beaufort, North Carolina. Each day the large boats cast off, hoping to return with a full catch of grouper, Spanish mackerel, tuna, wahoo, snapper, and an assortment of crabs and soft- shell crabs.

FISH AND SHELLFISH

Seafood is a natural part of summer vacations at the beach. This is the time when Southerners enjoy some of the most casual, relaxed meals of the year. After a long day on the Chesa- peake, beach-goers crack steamed crabs on newspaper-covered tables. In the Low Country, seafood boils are dumped out and shared as one-pot meals. And along the Gulf Coast, boiled shrimp drain in colanders while sunbathers peel 'em and eat 'em. There are no rules for summer seafood meals; almost anything goes, as long as there is plenty of ice-cold beer.

Boots Rutland's Crabmeat au Gratin

My husband's aunt shared this recipe one summer evening when we were visiting at her beach home on Perdido Bay. Fresh blue crabs were caught from the end of their pier and cracked and shelled in minutes. They ended up in this delicious casserole.

¼ cup unsalted butter or margarine
¼ cup all-purpose flour
¾ teaspoon salt
⅛ teaspoon black pepper
2 cups milk
1 teaspoon Worcestershire sauce
1 pound fresh blue crabmeat, drained
    and flaked
1 tablespoon unsalted butter or
    margarine, melted
½ cup soft fresh bread crumbs
¼ cup finely shredded Cheddar cheese
Paprika

Preheat oven to 350° F.

Melt ¼ cup butter; gradually add flour, salt, and pepper, stirring until smooth. Cook 1 minute, stirring constantly. Gradually add milk; cook over medium heat, stirring constantly, until thickened and bubbly. Stir in Worcestershire sauce and crabmeat. Cook, stirring constantly, until just heated through.

Spoon crabmeat mixture into individual baking shells or a lightly greased 1½-quart shallow baking dish. Bake for 15 minutes. Meanwhile, combine 1 tablespoon melted butter, bread crumbs, and cheese; sprinkle over casserole. Bake an additional 5 to 10 minutes, or until cheese melts and mixture is hot and bubbly. Sprinkle with paprika.

Yield: 4 servings.

Florida Grouper

Grouper is available from the Gulf Coast during the spring and summer months. Southerners have always considered this lean, firm, white fish to be a delicacy.

¹⁄₃ cup chopped green onions
¹⁄₄ cup unsalted butter or margarine, melted
¹⁄₄ cup orange juice
2 teaspoons grated orange rind
2 teaspoons soy sauce
¹⁄₂ teaspoon salt
4 grouper fillets (about 2 pounds)
2 oranges, peeled and cut into sections

Combine green onions, butter, orange juice, rind, soy sauce, and salt in a 13- x 9- x 2-inch baking dish. Place fillets in dish, turning to coat well. Cover and let stand 15 minutes.

Preheat oven to 350° F.

Turn fish in baking dish. Bake, uncovered, basting occasionally with pan juices, for 20 to 30 minutes, or until fish flakes easily when tested with a fork.

Transfer fillets to a serving platter. Add orange sections to pan juices, tossing well. Spoon over fillets. Serve immediately.

Yield: 4 servings.

Grouper is a versatile white fish; it makes excellent chowder, or it can be cut into fingers for frying. For an elegant touch, try baking grouper fillets in this citrus sauce of orange juice, soy sauce, green onions, and orange sections.

Uncle Jimmie's Boiled Shrimp with Cocktail Sauce

My Uncle Jimmie Callaway has perfected the art of boiling shrimp so that they come out moist and tender. Seafood experts in the coastal community of Panacea, Florida, have taught him that the secret lies in bringing the water to a boil before you add the shrimp. He also suggests rinsing the hot shrimp in cold water as soon as they are cooked.

2 quarts water
1 (3-ounce) package crab and shrimp
   boil
1 tablespoon salt
1 tablespoon cayenne pepper
2 bay leaves
2½ pounds unpeeled fresh shrimp
Cocktail sauce (recipe follows)

Combine 2 quarts water, crab and shrimp boil, salt, cayenne, and bay leaves in a large stockpot; bring to a boil. Reduce heat, and simmer 10 minutes. Add shrimp; cook 3 to 5 minutes, or just until shrimp turn pink. Drain well; rinse with cold water. Refrigerate until chilled. Peel and devein shrimp. Serve with cocktail sauce.

Yield: 6 servings.

Cocktail Sauce

1¼ cups chili sauce
3 tablespoons lemon juice
3 tablespoons prepared horseradish
2 teaspoons Worcestershire sauce
3 dashes hot sauce

Combine all ingredients, stirring until smooth. Cover and refrigerate at least 1 hour.

Yield: 1⅓ cups.

Low Country Seafood Boil

Miles of marshlands and sea islands and the winding shorelines of South Carolina and Georgia make up the area known as the Low Country. Since there is an emphasis on fish and seafood in this part of the South, casual outdoor gatherings will often include a large pot of shrimp, crabs, and vegetables boiled with special seasonings.

1 tablespoon salt
6 large potatoes, halved
5 large onions, peeled
3 (3-ounce) packages crab and shrimp boil
12 cloves garlic
5 lemons, halved
1 cup cider vinegar
1 dozen ears fresh corn, husks and silks removed
1 dozen live blue crabs
4 pounds unpeeled fresh shrimp
Cocktail Sauce (page 203)

Fill a 5-gallon stockpot or kettle two-thirds full of water; bring water to a boil. Add salt, potatoes, and onions; return to a boil. Cover stockpot and cook 20 minutes.

Add crab and shrimp boil, garlic, lemons, vinegar, corn, and crabs to stockpot. Cover and cook 10 minutes. Add shrimp; cover and cook 3 to 5 minutes, or just until pink.

Remove stockpot from heat; drain carefully. Arrange crab, shrimp, corn, onions, and potatoes on a large serving platter. Serve with cocktail sauce. Clean crabs and peel shrimp before eating.

Yield: 12 to 14 servings.

NOTE: Blue crabs are usually available in the South from April to October. If they are unavailable, increase shrimp to 5 pounds.

Opposite: Low Country Seafood Boil is a crowd pleaser. Just toss everything together in a stockpot, cook, drain, and serve.

When summer produce is at its peak, small vegetable stands spring up along roads throughout the South. The stands give farmers a chance to share their bounty with hungry customers.

VEGETABLES AND SALADS

Ask a Southerner about his summer vegetable garden and he'll show you rows of tomatoes, green beans, corn, cucumbers, eggplant, okra, and squash. He will point with pride to the twisting vines and stalks that, even early in the season, will be laden with young vegetables.

As the season heats up, meals turn lighter, and fresh vegetables are a natural. With such abundance, cooks often plan menus that feature "vegetable plates." A meal might consist of four to six different vegetables—simmered green beans, corn custard, eggplant casserole, fried okra, sliced tomatoes, and a square of corn bread.

Okra and Tomatoes

It is probable that okra was brought to our region by African slaves. Today, you can find okra growing during the summer months throughout the South. I like to harvest the prickly pods from tall green stalks and toss them into pots of simmering field peas or butter beans for added flavor. Dishes that make use of okra's thickening ability, such as the one below, are still popular in the South.

6 slices bacon
2 tablespoons all-purpose flour
4 cups sliced okra (about 1 pound)
1 cup chopped onion
½ cup chopped green bell pepper
2¾ cups chopped peeled tomato
½ teaspoon salt
½ teaspoon black pepper
¼ teaspoon cayenne pepper
Hot cooked rice (optional)

Cook bacon in a large skillet over medium heat until crisp. Remove bacon, reserving 2 tablespoons bacon drippings in skillet. Crumble bacon and set aside. Stir flour into reserved drippings and cook over medium heat, stirring constantly, until roux is caramel-colored (10 to 15 minutes). Add okra, onion, and green pepper; cook 2 minutes, stirring constantly. Stir in tomato, salt, pepper, and cayenne. Cover and simmer 15 minutes, or until okra is tender, stirring occasionally. Serve over rice, if desired. Sprinkle with reserved crumbled bacon.

Yield: 6 servings.

Few Southern children declare a fondness for okra, but it seems to become a favorite by the time they reach adulthood, especially when combined with tomatoes or other vegetables. Okra and Tomatoes is a classic recipe that represents true Southern cooking at its best.

Tangy Green Beans with Bacon

Like most Southerners, I love green beans made the old-fashioned way—flavored with bacon or ham hock and simmered for hours. But as a modern cook, I have also grown to appreciate the fresh flavor of green beans that have simmered for just a short time. This recipe has become one of my favorites because it features bacon flavor but retains the texture of the fresh green beans.

> 1 ¼ pounds fresh green beans
> 4 slices bacon
> 1 small onion, chopped
> ¾ cup sugar
> ½ cup cider vinegar

My mother used to "snap" her green beans, breaking them neatly and crisply into approximately 1-inch pieces, removing any strings in the process. But whether snapped or cut, Tangy Green Beans with Bacon are certain to turn out tender and tasty.

Remove strings from beans; wash beans and cut into 1-inch pieces. Set aside.

Cook bacon in a large skillet over medium-high heat until crisp; remove bacon, reserving drippings. Crumble bacon and set aside.

Sauté onion in bacon drippings until tender. Add sugar, stirring until sugar is dissolved. Stir in bacon, beans, and vinegar. Cover and bring to a boil; reduce heat and simmer 20 minutes, or just until beans are tender.

Yield: 4 to 6 servings.

Fried Okra

Some folks refuse to eat cooked okra because of its somewhat slimy quality. But when the pods are sliced, dredged in cornmeal and flour, and fried, a transformation takes place. Suddenly the okra becomes crisp and crunchy, and you will not be able to resist popping the tasty little morsels in your mouth.

> 1 ½ pounds fresh okra
> 2 eggs, beaten
> ⅓ cup buttermilk
> Vegetable oil for frying
> 1 cup all-purpose flour
> 1 cup cornmeal
> ½ teaspoon salt

I've seen fried okra served as a vegetable side dish and as an appetizer. With a sprinkling of salt, the crisp, crunchy morsels are consumed as fast as a bowl of popcorn.

Wash okra and cut into ¾-inch slices; pat dry with paper towels. Combine eggs and buttermilk in a large bowl; stir well. Add okra and let soak for 10 minutes. Drain.

Start heating vegetable oil for frying (375° F.).

Combine flour, cornmeal, and salt in a medium bowl. Dredge okra, a few pieces at a time, in flour mixture, coating well.

Fry okra in hot oil until golden. Drain on paper towels.

Yield: 6 to 8 servings.

Chilled Cucumber Soup

For many Southern gardeners, one of the rewards of all their toil and trouble is a refreshing bowl of cold cucumber soup. This soup not only tastes great, it looks pretty, too, and is the ideal accompaniment to a summer salad or sandwich.

> 3 cucumbers, peeled, seeded, and
>   chopped
> 2 cups sour cream
> 1 cup half-and-half
> 1 green onion, chopped
> 1 tablespoon lemon juice
> 2 teaspoons minced fresh dillweed or
>   ½ teaspoon dried dillweed
> ½ teaspoon garlic salt
> ¼ teaspoon white pepper

Combine all ingredients in container of an electric blender; process until smooth. Cover and refrigerate until thoroughly chilled.

Yield: 4 servings.

The flavor of Chilled Cucumber Soup benefits from just a hint of fresh dillweed.

Sweet Corn Custard

Fresh corn is one of the sweetest joys of summer. When cutting corn from the cob, use this rule of thumb: Two average-size ears of corn will yield about one cup of kernels.

> 2 cups fresh corn cut from cob (about 4 ears)
> 3 eggs, beaten
> ¾ cup (3 ounces) shredded Cheddar cheese
> ¼ cup all-purpose flour
> 4 teaspoons sugar
> ½ teaspoon salt
> ⅛ teaspoon black pepper
> ⅛ teaspoon ground nutmeg
> 2 cups half-and-half
> 2 tablespoons unsalted butter or margarine, melted

Preheat oven to 350° F.

Combine corn, eggs, and cheese in a large bowl, stirring well.

Combine flour, sugar, salt, pepper, and nutmeg; add to corn mixture. Stir in half-and-half and butter. Pour mixture into a lightly greased 1½-quart shallow baking dish. Place the dish in a 13- x 9- x 2-inch pan; add hot water to baking pan to a depth of 1 inch up sides of pan.

Bake, uncovered, for 1 hour, or until a knife inserted in center comes out clean.

Yield: 6 to 8 servings.

Simple Stuffed Squash

Yellow crookneck summer squash is usually plentiful if you have a summer garden. The mild-flavored squash is delicious stewed, steamed, fried, or baked. I like to prepare the recipe below for dinner guests because it looks so pretty on the plate. The squash are cooked whole, then cut in half and stuffed.

> 6 medium-size yellow squash
> 6 slices bacon
> 1 medium onion, chopped
> 1 tablespoon minced green bell pepper
> ½ cup chicken broth
> 1 cup fine dry bread crumbs
> ½ teaspoon salt
> ½ teaspoon black pepper
> ¼ cup unsalted butter or margarine, melted
> Parmesan cheese

When making Simple Stuffed Squash, it is best to cook the whole squash until it is tender but firm. This way the squash shell retains its shape when sliced in half.

Wash squash thoroughly. Place squash in boiling water to cover; simmer 10 to 15 minutes, or until tender but still firm. Drain and cool slightly. Trim off stems. Cut squash in half lengthwise; remove and reserve pulp, leaving a firm shell. Set aside.

Fry bacon over medium heat until crisp. Remove bacon, reserving 2 tablespoons drippings in skillet. Crumble bacon and set aside. Sauté onion and green pepper in drippings until tender.

Combine onion and green pepper with broth, bacon, bread crumbs, salt, pepper, and squash pulp; mix well. Place the squash shells in a lightly greased 13- x 9- x 2-inch baking dish. Spoon pulp mixture into shells; drizzle with butter and sprinkle with cheese. Broil about 3 minutes, or until lightly browned.

Yield: 6 servings.

Summer Gazpacho can be made ahead and kept in the refrigerator. The cool tomato-based soup makes a refreshing lunch or evening meal.

Summer Gazpacho

This cold soup originated in Spain, but it is perfect for hot Alabama evenings. My husband and I always try to stir up several batches of this flavorful soup when the fresh tomato crop reaches its peak.

4 cups tomato juice
3 cups peeled, chopped tomatoes

1 (10¾-ounce) can tomato soup, undiluted
1 cup peeled, chopped cucumber
¾ cup finely chopped green bell pepper
½ cup finely chopped green onion
⅓ cup bottled Italian salad dressing
2 cloves garlic, minced
2 tablespoons red wine vinegar
1 tablespoon lemon juice
¼ teaspoon salt
¼ teaspoon black pepper
⅛ teaspoon hot sauce

Garnish:

Croutons

Combine all ingredients with 1¼ cups water in a large bowl. Cover and refrigerate overnight. Ladle into soup bowls; garnish with croutons.

Yield: 10 cups.

Fried Green Tomatoes

Fried green tomatoes probably came into existence when an anxious gardener couldn't wait for his tomato crop to ripen, or when an overzealous cook was trying to use up the very last of the late summer tomatoes before a fall frost. Either way, a culinary hit was scored. It seems all Southerners are entranced with this cornmeal-coated treat.

> 1 cup cornmeal
> 2 teaspoons brown sugar
> ½ teaspoon salt
> ⅛ teaspoon black pepper
> 3 large green tomatoes, sliced
> 1 egg, beaten
> Vegetable oil for frying

Combine cornmeal, sugar, salt, and pepper in a small bowl; stir well. Dip tomato slices in beaten egg; dredge in cornmeal mixture, coating well on both sides.

Heat 2 to 3 tablespoons oil in a large cast-iron skillet over medium-high heat until hot. Add a layer of tomatoes; fry 3 to 5 minutes or until browned, turning once. Remove slices and drain. Repeat procedure, adding more oil to pan as needed, until all slices have been fried. Serve immediately.

Yield: 6 servings.

No other Southern vegetable dish has received as much attention as Fried Green Tomatoes. And every cook seems to have his or her own secret recipe; I like to add a little brown sugar to the cornmeal coating.

Tomato Aspic

Tomato aspic is the traditional dish to serve when the ladies come to lunch or bridge club. It is pretty presented as a large mold or cut into squares and served on lettuce leaves. My Aunt Alma had special tiny round salad molds that she always used for this tangy salad.

2 envelopes unflavored gelatin
2¼ cups tomato juice
2 tablespoons white vinegar
2 tablespoons lemon juice
¼ cup sugar
½ teaspoon salt
¼ teaspoon ground cloves
¼ teaspoon ground allspice
⅛ teaspoon black pepper
2 dashes hot sauce
⅓ cup diced green pepper
⅓ cup finely chopped celery
2 tablespoons minced onion
Lettuce leaves (optional)

Sprinkle gelatin over ½ cup cold water; let stand 1 minute.

Combine tomato juice, vinegar, lemon juice, sugar, salt, cloves, allspice, pepper, and hot sauce in a medium saucepan. Bring to a boil over medium heat. Add gelatin to hot tomato juice mixture; stir until gelatin dissolves. Chill until mixture is the consistency of unbeaten egg whites.

Fold in green pepper, celery, and onion. Pour mixture into a lightly oiled 4-cup mold; cover with plastic wrap and chill until firm. Unmold onto lettuce leaves, if desired.

Yield: 4 to 6 servings.

I've found that adding a small amount of green pepper, celery, and onion enhances the flavor and texture of Tomato Aspic.

Crimson Sweet, Charleston Gray, Dixie Queen, Jubilee, and Sugar Baby—even the names of Southern watermelons make your mouth water. Slice one open, and enjoy the sweet, juicy taste of summer.

DESSERTS

$\mathcal{S}$*outherners are passionate* about summer desserts. We look forward all year to enjoying fresh berries and peaches in pies and cobblers. The delicious blend of sweet bubbly fruit and pastry is the perfect way to end warm-weather meals.

When the weather gets too hot to bear, we cool things down with cold desserts. Tart limes add tropical flavor to a cool, creamy pie. And ice cream lovers sip thick milk shakes or refreshing punches that are sweet enough to end any meal.

Chilton County Peach Milk Shake

Chilton County lies between Birmingham and Montgomery, Alabama. This is the heart of Alabama peach country, and these folks make the best peach ice cream and peach milk shakes I have ever tasted. You will savor every sip of this creamy milk shake; it's thick with bits of juicy, ripe peaches.

1½ cups chopped fresh ripe peaches
1 tablespoon confectioners' sugar
1 cup milk
1½ cups vanilla or peach ice cream

Combine peaches and confectioners' sugar; toss gently. Refrigerate 1 to 6 hours. Combine peaches, milk, and ice cream in container of electric blender; process until smooth.

Yield: about 4 cups.

Chilton County Peach Milk Shake is made a bit sweeter by sprinkling the peeled, chopped peaches with a little confectioners' sugar. Blend the sweetened peaches with milk and peach or vanilla ice cream.

Cold Coffee Punch

Southerners have always been fond of coffee, but in the summer, you may find them sipping their brew cold rather than hot. I particularly like this coffee punch. It is thick and rich and sweet enough for dessert.

2 quarts hot strong brewed coffee
⅓ cup confectioners' sugar
2 cups milk
2 teaspoons vanilla extract
1 pint vanilla ice cream, softened
1 pint chocolate ice cream, softened
1½ cups heavy cream, whipped
Ground cinnamon

Combine coffee and confectioners' sugar, stirring until sugar dissolves. Refrigerate until thoroughly chilled.

Combine cold coffee mixture, milk, and vanilla; mix well. Scoop ice cream into a large punch bowl. Pour coffee mixture over ice cream, stirring gently. Top with dollops of whipped cream; sprinkle with cinnamon.

Yield: about 16 cups.

Summer Peach Cobbler

At least several times each summer, I buy enough peaches to make peach cobbler. There are many different recipes for this cobbler, but my favorite is very simple: just peaches flavored with vanilla and cinnamon, cooked until tender, and topped with a lattice pastry.

Summer Peach Cobbler is a special treat spooned up hot and topped with a scoop of vanilla ice cream.

Pastry:

1 ⅓ cups all-purpose flour
½ teaspoon salt
½ cup solid vegetable shortening
2 to 4 tablespoons cold water

Filling:

7 ½ to 8 cups sliced fresh peaches
1 ½ cups sugar
¼ cup flour
1 ½ teaspoons vanilla extract
½ teaspoon ground cinnamon
¼ cup unsalted butter or margarine, melted

To make the pastry, combine flour and salt; cut in shortening with a pastry blender until mixture resembles coarse meal. Sprinkle 2 to 4 tablespoons cold water, a tablespoon at a time, evenly over surface, stirring with a fork until all dry ingredients are moistened. Shape into a ball; chill.

To make the filling, combine peaches with other ingredients in a Dutch oven; set aside until mixture forms a syrup. Bring peaches to a boil; reduce heat, and cook, uncovered, 8 to 12 minutes, or until peaches are tender. Spoon peaches into a greased 11- x 7- x 2-inch baking dish.

Preheat oven to 475° F.

Roll out dough to ⅛-inch thickness on a lightly floured surface and cut into 1-inch strips; arrange in a lattice design over peaches. Bake for 15 minutes, or until golden.

Yield: 6 to 8 servings.

Key Lime Pie

Key limes are bright green, small, round, thin-skinned, and very tart. Persian limes are larger, oblong, bright green, seedless, less tart, and more frequently available in grocery stores. A true Key lime pie is made with Key lime juice and sweetened condensed milk; it has a regular pastry crust or a cookie-crumb crust and is often topped with whipped cream. Natives of the Florida Keys insist that the pie never be colored with green food coloring, as it often is in restaurants, but be left a natural pale yellow.

Single-Crust Pie Pastry (page 42)
4 egg yolks
½ cup Key lime juice
1 (14-ounce) can sweetened condensed milk
2 cups heavy cream
¼ cup sifted confectioners' sugar

Preheat oven to 450° F.

Line a 9-inch pie plate with pastry; trim and flute edges. Bake for 12 to 14 minutes, or until golden brown. Let cool completely.

Beat egg yolks with an electric mixer on medium speed until thick and lemon-colored. Heat juice in a saucepan over medium heat until thoroughly heated (about 160° F. on a candy thermometer). Gradually stir about one fourth of hot lime juice into yolks; add yolks to remaining hot lime juice in saucepan, stirring constantly. Cook 2 minutes, stirring constantly. Remove from heat and let cool. Add sweetened condensed milk, stirring until mixture becomes thick. Spoon filling into pie pastry, spreading evenly. Refrigerate until thoroughly chilled.

Beat cream with an electric mixer at high speed until foamy. Gradually add sugar, 1 tablespoon at a time, beating until stiff peaks form. Spoon whipped cream onto chilled pie. Refrigerate until serving time.

Yield: 6 to 8 servings.

This is essentially the same pie recipe that has been prepared in the Florida Keys for over a hundred years, except today the egg yolks are cooked before the sweetened condensed milk is added.

Summer Menus
Outdoor Hospitality

*B*rides marry throughout the year, but many choose the month of June for the wedding. Spring is waning into summer, and flowers burst fuller and sweeter. No wonder brides are sentimental about this time of year and the special events it brings, including the bridesmaids' luncheon, usually held the day before the wedding.

Close friends of the bride's mother will often host this event for the bride, her mother, attendants, sisters, and close relatives and friends. If the thermometer has not climbed to forbidding temperatures, the luncheon might be held on a shady porch or patio so the deep green leaves and summer flowers will echo the beauty of the tables.

BRIDESMAIDS' LUNCHEON

Cream of Yellow Squash Soup

Blue Crab and Wild Rice Salad

Minted Melon Toss

Green Bean and
New Potato Salad

Peppermint Ice Cream

White Wine Spritzers

Cream of Yellow Squash Soup

I have a fondness for cold soup. One of my favorite cold soups is this one, made with fresh yellow summer squash. It can be served casually from a mug or elegantly from a fine china cream soup bowl; either way, it will taste delicious. And if you happen to prefer your soup hot, then you will be pleased to know that this recipe can also be served immediately after cooking, before it is chilled.

2 tablespoons unsalted butter or
  margarine
1 tablespoon olive oil
⅓ cup minced onion
1 clove garlic, minced
1½ pounds yellow squash, thinly
  sliced
2 cups chicken broth
½ cup half-and-half
½ teaspoon salt
¼ teaspoon white pepper

Chicken broth and half-and-half form the base of this pastel-yellow vegetable soup.

Heat butter and oil in a large saucepan. Add onion and garlic; sauté over medium heat until tender. Stir in squash and chicken broth; cover and simmer 15 to 20 minutes, or until squash is tender.

Spoon half of squash mixture into container of an electric blender; process until smooth. Repeat with remaining squash mixture.

Return squash mixture to saucepan; stir in half-and-half, salt, and pepper. Cook over low heat, stirring constantly, until heated. Serve hot or cold.

Yield: 4 servings.

Blue Crab and Wild Rice Salad

The season for blue crabs runs from April to October. In Mobile, Alabama, West Indies Salad (crabmeat tossed with lemon juice, onion, and oil) is popular during this season. But I have always preferred this more colorful combination of crabmeat, wild rice, green peas, onions, and pimiento. This salad looks elegant served on a bed of lettuce or from a tomato shell.

1 (4-ounce) package wild rice
1 pound fresh blue crabmeat, drained and flaked
1¼ cups frozen tiny English peas, thawed
½ cup chopped green onions
1 (4-ounce) jar diced pimiento, drained
½ cup mayonnaise
½ cup sour cream
1 tablespoon lemon juice
1½ teaspoons curry powder
Tomato shell or lettuce leaves

Cook rice according to package directions; let cool. Combine rice, crabmeat, peas, green onions, and pimiento, stirring gently.

Combine mayonnaise, sour cream, lemon juice, and curry powder; add to crabmeat mixture, stirring gently. Serve in a tomato shell or over lettuce leaves.

Yield: 6 to 8 servings.

Minted Melon Toss

A sure way to set a pretty summer table is to include a large crystal bowl filled with cut-up watermelon, honeydew, and cantaloupe. A large watermelon can also be scooped out to hold the fruit.

1 cup sugar
2 cups lemon-lime carbonated soft drink
¼ cup loosely packed mint leaves
¼ cup lemon juice
3 cups watermelon balls
2 cups honeydew balls
1 cup cantaloupe balls

Combine sugar, lemon-lime drink, and mint leaves in a saucepan; stir well. Bring mixture to a boil over medium heat; boil 2 minutes, stirring constantly until sugar is dissolved, gently bruising mint leaves against sides of saucepan. Remove and discard mint leaves. Stir in lemon juice; cover and refrigerate.

Combine melon balls in a large bowl; pour syrup mixture over fruit and toss gently.

Yield: 6 servings.

Green Bean and New Potato Salad

Green beans, new potatoes, and cherry tomatoes are three vegetables that are often found in Southern backyard gardens. I think you will enjoy their fresh flavors when they are tossed together in a salad and dressed with a vinaigrette.

½ pound new potatoes, peeled and cubed
1 pound fresh green beans
10 cherry tomatoes, halved

Vinaigrette:
¼ cup olive oil
2 tablespoons white wine vinegar
2 tablespoons lemon juice
1 tablespoon finely chopped fresh basil or 1 teaspoon dried basil
½ teaspoon salt
¼ teaspoon garlic powder
¼ teaspoon coarsely ground black pepper

Cook potatoes in enough boiling water to cover for 15 minutes, or until just tender. Drain, and set aside.

Remove strings from beans. Cut beans into 1½-inch pieces. Wash thoroughly. Cover beans with water and bring to a boil. Reduce heat, cover, and simmer 8 to 10 minutes or until crisp-tender. Drain.

Combine potatoes, beans, and tomatoes in a large bowl, tossing gently. Combine vinaigrette ingredients in a small bowl, stirring vigorously; pour dressing over vegetables. Toss gently. Cover and refrigerate at least 4 hours.

Yield: 4 to 6 servings.

The flavors, textures, and colors of Blue Crab and Wild Rice Salad, Minted Melon Toss, and Green Bean and New Potato Salad team nicely to create a lovely luncheon plate.

Peppermint Ice Cream

It is no wonder that my husband has a special fondness for peppermint ice cream—his mother has one of the finest recipes I have ever sampled. She starts with a sweet custard base and stirs in crushed hard peppermint candy.

5 cups milk
1¾ cups sugar
¼ cup plus 2 tablespoons all-purpose
   flour
5 eggs, beaten
1 cup crushed hard peppermint candy
4 cups half-and-half

Heat milk in a 3-quart saucepan over low heat until thoroughly heated (about 180° F. on a candy thermometer) but not boiling. Combine sugar and flour; gradually add sugar mixture to milk, stirring until blended. Cook over medium heat, stirring constantly, 15 to 20 minutes, or until slightly thickened.

Gradually stir one fourth of hot mixture into beaten eggs; add eggs to remaining hot mixture, stirring constantly. Cook 1 minute. Remove from heat; stir in crushed candy. Cover and refrigerate mixture until candy has dissolved (about 2 hours). Stir in half-and-half.

Pour custard mixture into freezer can of a 1-gallon hand-turned or electric ice cream freezer. Freeze according to manufacturer's instructions. Let ripen 1½ to 2 hours.

Yield: 1 gallon.

Peppermint Ice Cream is made by allowing crushed peppermint candy to melt in a thick, sweet custard sauce. The ice cream may have a delicate appearance, but it is packed with lusty peppermint flavor.

*S*outherners always leap at the opportunity to have a picnic during the hot summer months. Although summer does not officially begin until late June, its spirit permeates Memorial Day. After that, people plan family get-togethers, high school reunions, and Fourth of July and Labor Day cookouts, often heading for the park to celebrate.

Swings, slides, and merry-go-rounds provide instant entertainment in conveniently located neighborhood parks. State parks, within easy driving distance of towns and cities, boast lakes and beaches for splashing, fishing, or boating.

The more this excitement stimulates appetites, the more attention the food receives. But on hot days, always remember to store perishables in insulated coolers with plenty of ice. Don't serve the meal until everyone is ready to eat, and return the leftover food to the coolers as soon as the crowd has finished eating.

PICNIC IN THE PARK

Deviled Eggs

Picnic Fried Chicken

Potato Salad

Butter Bean Salad

Okra Pickles

Lemon Angel Food Cake

Shade Tree Lemonade

Deviled Eggs

I think it is traditional that all Southern brides receive a deviled-egg plate as a wedding gift. An aunt gave me one of these unique plates when I married, and I must admit that I have found the dish helpful in transporting deviled eggs to picnics or when serving the eggs at luncheons.

6 hard-cooked eggs
¼ cup mayonnaise
2 tablespoons chopped sweet pickles
1 tablespoon chopped green olives
1 teaspoon cider vinegar
1 teaspoon prepared mustard
¼ teaspoon salt
⅛ teaspoon black pepper
Paprika

Slice eggs in half lengthwise, and carefully remove yolks. Mash yolks with mayonnaise in a bowl. Add remaining ingredients except paprika and stir well. Spoon yolk mixture into egg whites. Sprinkle stuffed eggs with paprika.

Yield: 6 servings.

The egg yolks of these hard-cooked eggs are mashed and combined with pickles, olives, vinegar, and mustard for spicy deviled flavor.

Picnic Fried Chicken

When it comes to Southern fried chicken, recipes vary from state to state, and within each neighborhood and family. Some cooks just dredge their chicken in seasoned flour, while others soak the bird in buttermilk first. As for frying, some cooks feel that covering with the skillet lid will assure even cooking; others swear that an open skillet gives the chicken a crisper coating.

1¼ cups all-purpose flour
1 teaspoon salt
½ teaspoon black pepper
1 cup buttermilk
1 (2½- to 3-pound) broiler-fryer,
    cut up
Vegetable oil for frying

Combine flour, salt, and pepper in a large bowl, stirring well. Pour buttermilk into a deep bowl; dip each piece of chicken in buttermilk and dredge in flour mixture, coating well.

Heat 1 inch of vegetable oil in a large cast-iron or electric skillet to 350° F.

Picnic Fried Chicken tastes just as good cold as it does hot. The outside might be crisp and brown, but inside, each piece is moist and tender.

Place chicken in hot oil and cook until browned, turning to brown both sides. Reduce heat until temperature of oil is lowered to 275°, cover chicken and cook 20 minutes. Uncover and cook an additional 5 minutes. Drain on paper towels.

Yield: 4 servings.

Potato Salad

I wouldn't consider going on a picnic without bringing lots of potato salad. This classic Southern dish typically contains potatoes, hard-cooked eggs, celery, pickles, and onions.

8 large red potatoes, peeled and cubed
2 hard-cooked eggs, chopped
½ cup chopped celery

⅓ cup sweet pickle relish
¼ cup chopped green onions
1 (2-ounce) jar diced pimiento, drained
½ cup mayonnaise
½ cup sour cream
1 teaspoon prepared mustard
½ teaspoon salt
¼ teaspoon black pepper

Cook potatoes in boiling salted water to cover for 20 minutes, or until tender. Drain and cool slightly. Combine potatoes, eggs, celery, pickle relish, onions, and pimiento in a large bowl, tossing gently.

Combine mayonnaise, sour cream, mustard, salt, and pepper, stirring well; add to vegetable mixture, tossing gently.

Yield: 6 to 8 servings.

It is best to use waxy boiling potatoes when making Potato Salad; they contain less starch and are more moist than baking potatoes, and will not crumble when ingredients are tossed.

Butter Bean Salad

During the summer months, my mother would often spend the hot, humid evenings shelling pale green or speckled butter beans—baby lima beans. The next day, we would always sit down to a large bowl of these flavorful beans, which had been cooked with ham hock or salt pork. Afterward, a cold salad, such as the one below, could be prepared.

4 cups cooked butter beans, drained
½ cup chopped celery
2 green onions, chopped
2 hard-cooked eggs, coarsely chopped
¼ cup chopped green bell pepper
1 (2-ounce) jar diced pimiento,
  drained
2 tablespoons chopped fresh parsley
½ cup mayonnaise
Lettuce leaves

Combine beans, celery, onions, eggs, green pepper, pimiento, and parsley, tossing gently. Stir in mayonnaise. Cover and refrigerate at least several hours.

Serve salad over lettuce leaves.

Yield: 4 to 6 servings.

Most old-time Southerners refer to baby lima beans as "butter beans." The beans are picked and sold in their pods, which should be plump, firm, and dark green. The fresh beans are shelled just before using, although the shelled beans might be frozen and used later.

Okra Pickles

These tangy pickles are especially popular in the South. Some folks like to serve the pickles straight from the jar, while others prefer to serve them from a beautiful crystal dish or silver tray. If you have never tried okra pickles, you will be surprised, for they are crisp and flavorful and make a delightful appetizer.

3½ pounds small okra pods
14 cloves garlic
7 small fresh red or green chili peppers
1 quart water
1 pint white vinegar (5% acidity)
⅓ cup pickling salt
1 tablespoon dillseeds

Wash okra thoroughly. Pack okra tightly into 7 hot sterilized pint jars; place 2 garlic cloves and a hot pepper in each jar. Combine 1 quart water, the vinegar, pickling salt, and dillseeds in a saucepan; bring to a boil. Pour boiling vinegar mixture over okra, leaving ½-inch headspace. Remove air bubbles; wipe jar rims. Cover at once with metal lids and screw on bands. Process in boiling-water bath for 10 minutes.

Yield: 7 pints.

Cloves of garlic, hot peppers, and dillseeds add plenty of zesty flavor to Okra Pickes.

Lemon Angel Food Cake

There are tales that this light, airy sponge-type cake originated in India. However, many Southerners prefer to believe that a frugal ancestor created the cake in order to avoid discarding egg whites left over from other baking projects.

12 egg whites
1¼ teaspoons cream of tartar
Pinch of salt
1½ cups sugar
1 cup sifted cake flour
1 teaspoon lemon extract
½ teaspoon vanilla extract

Preheat oven to 350° F.

Beat egg whites with an electric mixer on high speed until foamy. Add cream of tartar and salt; beat until soft peaks form. Add sugar, 2 tablespoons at a time, beating until stiff peaks form. Sprinkle flour over egg-white mixture, ¼ cup at a time, folding in carefully each time. Fold in flavorings.

Pour batter into an ungreased 10-inch tube pan, spreading evenly. Bake for 35 to 45 minutes, or until cake springs back when lightly touched. Remove cake from oven and immediately invert pan; let cool at least 1 hour. Remove cake from pan.

Yield: one 10-inch cake.

Lemon Angel Food Cake should be baked in an ungreased tube pan; this allows the batter to cling to the sides and rise higher. The cake should also be cooled upside down to prevent shrinking and falling. For best results, invert the hot pan over the neck of a bottle so air can circulate beneath it.

Shade Tree Lemonade

A summer afternoon in the South can get mighty hot and humid. These are the times when nothing can quench the thirst better than a big glass of freshly made lemonade. Almost every home-maker has her own recipe for this drink. On special occasions it might be tinted pink with cherry juice or red food coloring.

1 ½ cups sugar
½ cup water
Grated rind of 1 lemon
1 ½ cups fresh lemon juice
4 ½ cups ice water

Combine sugar and ½ cup water in a small saucepan; place over low heat and stir until sugar dissolves. Remove from heat and let mixture cool. Add lemon rind, lemon juice, and ice water; mix well. Refrigerate until thoroughly chilled. Serve over ice.

Yield: about 7 cups.

The sugar syrup base for Shade Tree Lemonade can be made ahead and kept on hand in the refrigerator.

Every July Fourth, Americans celebrate one of their well-loved holidays, the country's birthday. Although some like to parade on flag-lined boulevards, many Southerners slip away to the lake or river for a family gathering. If the holiday falls near the weekend, it becomes a three- or four-day vacation, and all the more jubilantly enjoyed. Most of the family will laze away the day, soaking up the sun between dips in the water. But the fishermen are called to duty: to bring home the fish for an afternoon fish fry.

FOURTH OF JULY
FISH FRY

Delta Fried Catfish

Baked Beans

Country Coleslaw

Fried Onion Rings

Mama's Crisp Sweet Pickles

Marinated Tomatoes
and Cucumbers

Hush Puppies ♦ Watermelon

Peach Ice Cream ♦ Iced Tea

Delta Fried Catfish

As a child, I can remember making regular visits to a Bainbridge, Georgia, catfish "house" where they served up enormous platters of deep-fried channel catfish, fresh from the Flint River. These days, farmers in Mississippi have turned to raising catfish as a commercial crop. To celebrate their success, the World Catfish Festival is held each year in Belzoni, Mississippi.

Vegetable oil for frying
6 whole, cleaned catfish (4 to 5
*   pounds)*
3 cups cornmeal
1¼ teaspoons salt
2½ cups buttermilk

Start oil heating to 350° F. in a large, deep skillet.

Rinse fish under cold water; pat dry and set aside.

Combine cornmeal and salt in a large bowl. Dip fish in buttermilk and dredge in cornmeal mixture.

Fry fish, several at a time, until they float to top and are golden brown. Drain well. Serve immediately.

Yield: 6 servings.

No Southern fish fry would be complete without a generous helping of cornmeal-coated Delta Fried Catfish and Hush Puppies.

Baked Beans

This is a simple baked beans recipe that I have been using for years. It is a great choice to take to covered-dish dinners, and it is an absolute must whenever you plan a fish fry or barbecue.

2 (16-ounce) cans pork and beans
¾ cup firmly packed brown sugar
½ cup chopped onion
½ cup catsup
¼ cup chopped green bell pepper
2 teaspoons prepared mustard
4 slices bacon
1 green bell pepper, cut into thin rings

Preheat oven to 350° F.

Combine all ingredients, except bacon and pepper rings; stir well. Spoon into a lightly greased 2-quart baking dish. Arrange bacon slices and pepper rings over top. Bake, uncovered, for 1 hour.

Yield: 6 servings.

This traditional coleslaw is combined with mayonnaise and a little pickle relish for just a hint of sweetness.

Country Coleslaw

Fried fish and hush puppies go hand in hand with this creamy coleslaw. A small amount of shredded red cabbage can be stirred in for more color.

1 small cabbage, shredded
1½ cups shredded carrots

½ cup diced green bell pepper
½ cup sweet pickle relish
¾ to 1 cup mayonnaise
1 tablespoon sugar
½ teaspoon salt

Combine cabbage, carrots, green pepper, and pickle relish in a large bowl; toss gently to combine.

Combine mayonnaise, sugar, and salt; stir well. Pour mixture over cabbage, tossing gently to combine. Cover and refrigerate at least 30 minutes, or until serving time.

Yield: 10 servings.

Baked Beans are a simple-to-make addition to any casual menu.

Fried Onion Rings

You probably don't want to eat a large helping of fried onion rings at every meal, but they certainly are good served with fish or hamburgers. Some cooks like to coat their onion rings in a beer-and-flour batter, but I prefer soaking the rings in ice water for extra crispness, then coating them in a buttermilk batter.

2 large Spanish or Vidalia onions
Vegetable oil for frying
2¼ cups all-purpose flour
1 tablespoon cornmeal
1½ teaspoons baking powder
1 teaspoon salt
2 cups buttermilk
2 eggs, separated

Peel onions; cut into ½-inch-thick slices, and separate into rings. Place rings in a large bowl of ice water. Let stand 30 minutes; drain on paper towels.

Start heating oil to 375° F. in a large, deep skillet.

Place drained onion rings in a large plastic or paper bag; add 1 cup of the flour, and shake until rings are coated.

Combine remaining 1¼ cups flour, cornmeal, baking powder, salt, and buttermilk; stir in egg yolks, mixing well. Beat egg whites until stiff peaks form; fold into batter.

Dip onion rings in batter, coating well. Fry onion rings, a few at a time, in the hot oil for 3 to 5 minutes, or until golden brown. Drain on paper towels. Serve immediately.

Yield: 4 to 6 servings.

A buttermilk batter, made fluffy with beaten egg whites, gives Fried Onion Rings a light, golden coating.

Mama's Crisp Sweet Pickles

My father has a beautiful vegetable garden. The vegetables get lots of attention and care throughout every season, but especially during the humid summer months. Each year he produces a prolific cucumber crop, which my mother turns into these pickles. The slices are so crisp that they seem to snap when you bite into them.

For a more attractive appearance, cucumbers can be sliced with a crinkle cutter when making Mama's Crisp Sweet Pickles.

7 pounds small cucumbers
2 gallons water
2 cups pickling lime
2 quarts crushed ice
8 cups white vinegar (5% acidity)
8 cups sugar
1 tablespoon salt
2 teaspoons mixed pickling spices

Wash cucumbers and slice into ¼-inch-thick slices. Combine cucumber slices, 2 gallons water, and pickling lime in a large crockery bowl; let soak for 12 hours. Drain cucumber slices and rinse in cold water; repeat draining and rinsing procedure three times (to remove lime). Pack crushed ice over cucumbers; cover and let stand 4 hours. Drain well.

Heat vinegar, sugar, salt, and pickling spices in a large saucepan, stirring constantly, until mixture comes to a boil and sugar dissolves. Pour syrup mixture over cucumbers; let stand 5 to 6 hours or overnight.

Bring cucumber-and-syrup mixture to a boil; reduce heat, and simmer 35 minutes. Pack into hot sterilized jars, leaving ½-inch headspace. Remove air bubbles; wipe jar rims. Cover at once with metal lids and screw on bands. Process in boiling-water bath for 10 minutes.

Yield: about 8 pints.

Marinated Tomatoes and Cucumbers

Tomatoes and cucumbers appear in all sorts of Southern salads, but I think the combination is especially happy when vegetables are marinated in a tangy vinegar and dillweed dressing. This salad can be made ahead and stored in the refrigerator, which makes it perfect for serving on hot summer evenings.

3 large tomatoes, sliced
1 large cucumber, thinly sliced
½ cup cider vinegar
½ cup vegetable oil
1 teaspoon sugar
1 teaspoon dried thyme or dillweed
½ teaspoon salt
½ teaspoon black pepper
Lettuce leaves

Place tomato slices and cucumber slices in a large shallow container. Combine vinegar, oil, sugar, thyme, salt, and pepper; stir well and pour over vegetables. Cover and refrigerate at least 2 hours. Just before serving, remove tomatoes and cucumbers with a slotted spoon, and arrange on lettuce leaves. Spoon on remaining marinade, if desired.

Yield: 6 servings.

Hush Puppies

I have always heard that hush puppies were created in the fishing camps along the coast of north Florida. While camp cooks were frying fish, they would throw scraps of fried batter to barking dogs and yell, "Hush, Puppies!"

1 cup cornmeal
½ cup all-purpose flour
1 ½ teaspoons baking powder
1 teaspoon salt
1 teaspoon sugar
¼ teaspoon garlic powder
¼ teaspoon black pepper
⅛ teaspoon cayenne pepper
1 egg, beaten
⅔ cup milk
⅓ cup minced onion
Vegetable oil for frying

Combine dry ingredients in a large bowl. Add egg, milk, and onion, stirring just until dry ingredients are moistened. Let batter stand 3 to 5 minutes.

While batter is standing, start heating oil to 375° F. in a large, deep skillet.

Drop batter by rounded tablespoonfuls into hot oil. Fry, turning once, for 3 to 5 minutes, or until hush puppies float to top of oil and are golden brown. Drain well on paper towels.

Yield: about 1 ½ dozen.

Peach Ice Cream

When I was a child I attended several summer gatherings where everyone would take a turn at churning the ice cream. The hand-turned freezer was always heavy and cantankerous, and we were constantly having to add more ice or salt. But nobody ever dared to complain, because we all knew what a delicious reward awaited us. Just the thought of those juicy peaches swimming in vanilla cream made you want to churn a little faster.

4½ cups mashed fresh ripe peaches
2¼ cups sugar
3 eggs
¼ cup all-purpose flour
¼ teaspoon salt
3½ cups milk
2 cups half-and-half
1 cup heavy cream
1 tablespoon vanilla extract

Combine peaches and ¾ cup of the sugar; stir well and set aside.

Beat eggs with an electric mixer on medium speed until frothy. Combine remaining 1½ cups sugar, flour, and salt; stir well. Gradually add sugar mixture to eggs; beat until slightly thickened. Add milk; mix well.

Pour egg mixture into a large saucepan. Cook over low heat, stirring constantly, until mixture thickens enough to coat a metal spoon (about 15 minutes). Cover and refrigerate mixture until thoroughly chilled (about 2 hours). Stir in half-and-half, cream, vanilla, and reserved peaches.

Pour mixture into freezer container of a 1-gallon hand-turned or electric freezer. Freeze according to manufacturer's instructions. Let ripen 1 to 2 hours before serving.

Yield: about 1 gallon.

Mashed fresh peaches and vanilla extract are stirred into a sweet custard base to make Peach Ice Cream.

Index